English for the Real World

LIVING LANGUAGE®

A Random House Company

English
for the
Real World

Andrea Penruddocke

Christopher A. Warnasch

INTERMEDIATE
ESL

Published in the United States by Living Language, A Random House Company

www.livinglanguage.com

Editor: Suzanne McQuade
Production Editor: John Whitman
Production Managers: Helen Kilcullen and Heather Lanigan
Interior Design: Sophie Ye Chin

First Edition
ISBN 1-4000-2087-5

Library of Congress Cataloging-in-Publication Data available upon request.

PRINTED IN THE UNITED STATES OF AMERICA

10 9 8 7 6 5 4

Acknowledgments

Thanks to the Living Language staff: Tom Russell, Elizabeth Bennett, Christopher Warnasch, Zviezdana Verzich, Suzanne McQuade, Helen Tang, Sophie Chin, Denise De Gennaro, Linda Schmidt, Alison Skrabek, John Whitman, Arlene Aizer, Helen Kilcullen, and Heather Lanigan.

Contents

Introduction

WELCOME TO *ENGLISH FOR THE REAL WORLD*! This intermediate-level English course was designed by the experts at Living Language® specifically to meet the needs of people who speak and understand English well enough to get by, but who would like to improve their grammar, expand their vocabulary, and refine their pronunciation and listening comprehension. *English for the Real World* combines practical real life situations such as interviewing for a job or renting an apartment with precisely the grammar and vocabulary that intermediate-level students of English need. In short, if you'd like to speak English more naturally—the way it's really spoken—then this course is perfect for you.

Here's how it works. Each of the twenty lessons will cover a topic that you are most likely deal with in your own life—everything from working to doing household chores to shopping to going to a party. And each lesson is divided into four basic parts:

DIALOGUE: The first section of each lesson will be a dialogue that puts you into the situation. Read through the dialogue in the book, and listen to it on the CDs that come with this course. You'll first hear the dialogue at normal, conversational speed, and then once again at a slower speed, with pauses for repetition. Listen and repeat carefully—this will help make your pronunciation and intonation more natural, and it will also improve your speaking proficiency.

WORDS IN ACTION: After you've listened to the dialogue a second time, you'll have a chance to review the vocabulary and idiomatic expressions that you came across in the dialogue. You'll see a list of words and example sentences that are from the dialogue or related to the lesson topic. You may know some, or even most, of the words, but this section is your chance to see how they're used in natural conversational English. Read through the list and the examples to see how to put those words into action. After you've read the list a few times and become familiar with individual words and phrases, turn on your CD again. All of the words and examples in **_bold italics_** are on your CDs so you can practice your pronunciation and intonation further. Finally, you'll get another chance to practice the vocabulary before you move on.

TAKE A CLOSER LOOK: The third section of each lesson will offer an opportunity to look closely at some of the structures used in the dialogue and elsewhere in the lesson. You'll see a lot of grammar that you probably can understand easily enough, but that you may need some help using on your own. That's the whole point of this section— you can stop and take a closer look at the structures that intermediate-level English students sometimes find confusing. You'll see easy explanations written in plain English, and plenty of examples from real life. You'll also have plenty of opportunities to practice. Some material from this section may be a review for you, but they're all helpful, and once you're in command of these points, your English will become more fluent and natural. Portions of these sections are on your CDs; follow the symbols to play and pause these examples.

LISTENING EXERCISE: The last section of each lesson will help you build your listening and speaking skills even more. You'll hear an interactive exercise on the CD that will give you the chance to speak your answers rather than write them. The exercise will highlight one of the points from the lesson itself—vocabulary, structure, idiomatic expressions—and help you practice using that point in lively, authentic spoken English.

Learning the basics of English is difficult and has its own challenges. Luckily, you've already made it through that. This course is designed to help you master English and sound more natural and fluent. And best of all you can use it at your own pace. Don't be afraid to go back over the lessons you're uncomfortable with to make sure you've had plenty of practice. Because that's the most important part of sounding natural—practice.

Good luck!

KEY TO SYMBOLS

When you see the 🎧, PLAY CD and listen to the examples or exercises on the audio portion of the course.

When you see the 📖, PAUSE CD and return to the book until you see the next 🎧.

English for the Real World

Lesson 1

DEPARTURE AND ARRIVAL

In this lesson you'll read and listen to a dialogue about Mr. Thabo, a South African man who is flying from Johannesburg to New York. You'll learn vocabulary and expressions useful for airports, customs and immigration, renting a car, and travel in general. You'll also review different uses of the continuous tenses of verbs, or the *-ing* forms, such as *was going* or *am sitting* or *will be taking*. As with every lesson in this course, you'll have plenty of chances to practice and review what you've learned, and if you're not ready to move on, you can re-read the text or listen to the recordings as many times as you'd like.

1A DIALOGUE

WHERE WILL YOU BE FLYING TODAY?

Mr. Thabo is traveling from Johannesburg, South Africa, to New York City. Let's listen as he checks in at the ticket counter. First, read through the dialogue once. Then listen to it at normal conversational speed. You'll have a chance to listen and repeat later.

Attendant:	*Where will you be flying today?*
Mr. Thabo:	*New York.*
Attendant:	*May I see your ticket, passport, and visa, please?*
Mr. Thabo:	*Here you go. My visa's on page six of my passport.*
Attendant:	*Would you like a window or an aisle seat?*
Mr. Thabo:	*Aisle, please.*
Attendant:	*Do you prefer smoking, or non-smoking?*
Mr. Thabo:	*Non-smoking.*
Attendant:	*I have 13E available. How many pieces of luggage do you have?*
Mr. Thabo:	*Two.*
Attendant:	*Here's your boarding pass. The plane will board half an hour prior to departure. You'll be leaving from gate three, on your left.*
Mr. Thabo:	*Thank you.*

Now listen to the dialogue again. This time, repeat after the native speakers in the pauses provided.

Now Mr. Thabo has arrived in New York, and he's going through immigration. Again, you'll hear the dialogue first at normal, conversational speed. Then you'll hear it again with pauses so that you can repeat what you hear.

Announcement:	*Welcome to John F. Kennedy International Airport. Please have your passport and immigration forms ready.*
Immigration Official:	*What's the purpose of your visit? Business or pleasure?*
Mr. Thabo:	*Pleasure.*
Immigration Official:	*How long will you be staying in the United States?*
Mr. Thabo:	*Three months.*
Immigration Official:	*OK. Please proceed to customs.*
	(AT CUSTOMS)
Customs Official:	*Do you have dairy or meat products with you?*
Mr. Thabo:	*No.*
Customs Official:	*OK, you're all set.*

Listen to the dialogue a second time, and repeat in the pauses provided.

Finally, Mr. Thabo has gone through passport control and customs, he's picked up his luggage, and he's ready to go from the airport into the city. He could take a train, a bus, or a taxi, but since he's staying in the US for three months, he decides to rent a car for a week instead to take a look around. Let's listen.

Mr. Thabo:	*Hi. I'd like to rent a car for a week.*
Agent:	*What kind would you like?*
Mr. Thabo:	*A compact.*
Agent:	*May I see your driver's license?*
Mr. Thabo:	*Will my international license do?*
Agent:	*Sure. Just fill out this form. Write your address here and sign your name on the bottom of the page. Unlimited mileage and the mandatory collision insurance are included.*
Mr. Thabo:	*Do I have to return the car to this location?*
Agent:	*No, you can drop it off at any of our local branches.*
Mr. Thabo:	*The keys are in the car?*
Agent:	*Yes. Our complimentary bus to the parking lot is through the door to your right.*
Mr. Thabo:	*Great!*

Listen once more to the dialogue, and repeat in the pauses provided.

1B WORDS IN ACTION

Now let's go back and review some of the vocabulary that you heard in the dialogues. Remember that the words and expressions in bold are on your recordings to help you practice your pronunciation. First, however, read through all of the vocabulary and practice aloud.

window seat
I'd like a window seat so I can watch the landing.

aisle
The flight attendant is standing in the aisle.

smoking section
I have to sit in the smoking section because my wife smokes.
Many restaurants do not have smoking sections.

available
Are there any tickets available for the opera tomorrow night?
Is Mrs. Ramirez available for an appointment on Tuesday, February 18?

prior to
She has to buy all of her books prior to the first day of classes; she needs them before the class starts.
You have to arrive at the airport at least two hours prior to your flight.

immigration forms
Be sure to use a pen when filling out the immigration forms.

proceed
After going through passport control, the passengers proceeded to customs.

dairy
Milk, yogurt, and cheese are all dairy products.

you're all set
All I need is your signature, and you're all set to go.
I was all set to leave the house, but the phone rang.

compact
I don't need a big car; a compact will do.
Laptop computers have become very compact; the older ones used to be bigger.

unlimited mileage
With unlimited mileage, you don't have to pay extra for every mile you drive.

mandatory
You have to take collision insurance; it's mandatory.

included
The tip is not included in your bill; you have to leave the waiter extra money.

drop off
I asked the taxi driver to drop me off at Fifth Avenue and 43rd Street.
He dropped off his laundry in the morning, and he'll pick it up in the evening.

branch
This isn't our only branch office; we have branches all over the United States.
Her company opened a branch office in Cape Town.

Now turn on the recording and listen to the vocabulary in bold. Repeat each word or expression, and the example sentence, in the pauses provided.

PRACTICE: VOCABULARY

Are you familiar with all of the vocabulary from this lesson? If not, go back and listen again. If you're ready to practice what you've learned, fill in the blanks in each of the following sentences using the words and expressions listed below. Each word or expression will only be used once.

window seat	smoking section	prior to
aisle	available	immigration forms

proceed   compact   included
dairy   unlimited   drop...off
all set   mandatory   branch

1. I want to buy a new, _____ laptop. My old one is too big and bulky.
2. Departing passengers must go through security _____ _____ arriving at their gates.
3. You need a license to drive; it's _____.
4. He works for the same company, but at a different _____ in another city.
5. The girl cannot drink milk because she's allergic to _____ products.
6. You take the _____ _____ so that you can see when we take off and land.
7. I prefer the _____ seat so that I can stand up and move more easily.
8 He couldn't make a reservation at the restaurant because there were no tables _____.
9. We must not act as if there were an _____ supply of energy.
10. Could you _____ me _____ at my house?
11. Is the tax _____ in that price, or is it extra?
12. Now it's against the law to have a _____ _____ in restaurants in this city. People have to smoke outside.
13. Okay, you're _____ _____ to leave right after you pay the bill.
14. _____ to checkout if you've found everything you need.
15. Make sure you have all of your _____ _____ ready before you go through passport control and customs.

1C TAKE A CLOSER LOOK

In this section of each lesson we'll go back and take a closer look at some of the structures or idioms you heard used in the dialogues.

QUESTION WORDS
First, let's talk about asking questions. Before we begin, turn the CD on and listen to some examples of questions.

🎧 *Where will you be flying today?*
Does she speak English?
Are we leaving today?

📖 As you know, there are a few different ways to form questions in English. Let's start with question words. Remember: *who, what, which, where, when, how, how much, how many, why.*

Who is the pilot for our flight?
What did the flight attendant say?

Which gate do we leave from?
Where is the baggage claim area?
When does the flight leave?
How do I get to Terminal B?
Why is the flight delayed?
How much more time does it take to fly to Philadelphia?
How many pieces of carry-on luggage may I take?

Take a look again at the last two questions. Remember to use *how much?* when asking about things that you cannot count—time, money, coffee, snow, freedom. Use *how many?* for items that you can count—minutes, dollars, cups of coffee, snowflakes, children, houses.

How many cups of coffee do you want?
How much sugar do you take in your coffee?

PRACTICE: QUESTION WORDS
Fill in the blank with one of the question words provided.

1. _____ is the woman who is sitting next to you on the plane?
    (What/Who/Why)
2. _____ are you flying into Philadelphia and not New York?
    (Where/What/Why)
3. _____ can we use our mobile phones on the plane?
    (When/Who/Which)
4. _____ are you getting into the city, by bus or by taxi?
    (What/When/How)
5. _____ flights are there to San Francisco today? (How much/How many)
6. _____ is the security check point? (Where/Who/How)
7. _____ do you take in your tea? (Who/How/What)
8. Do you know _____ you want to go for dinner tonight?
    (where/why/how many)
9. I can't decide _____ seat I prefer, the aisle or the window.
    (how/which/who)
10. The flight attendant explained _____ we were waiting on the runway.
    (which/who/why)
11. Can you tell me _____ the flight for Santo Domingo leaves?
    (who/what/when)
12. _____ is that talking to the captain? (Who/What/Where)
13. _____ did I leave my car keys? (What/Where/Who)
14. _____ time do we have before we have to leave? (How much/How many)
15. _____ did you get from the airport to the city? (Where/Which/How)

FORMING QUESTIONS

Turn on the recording and listen to the following two sentences.

🎧 *The keys are in the car.*
The keys are in the car?

📖 As you can hear, you can form a question in English just by changing your intonation. All you have to do is raise the intonation at the end of the question. Of course, that's just one way to form a question. The more common way to form a question in English is to change the position of the verb.

Take a look at these examples:

The man is buying a round-trip ticket to Buenos Aires.
It will take seven hours to arrive there.
The plane has already left the gate.
The children were sleeping during the flight.
She would fly first class if she had the money.
They will be traveling in business class.

In each of these statements, the verb is made of more than one word (*is buying, will take, has left, were sleeping, would fly, will be traveling*). To make questions out of these statements, put the first word of the verb in the first position in the sentence. For example:

Is the man buying a round-trip ticket to Buenos Aires?
Will it take seven hours to arrive there?
Has the plane already left the gate?
Were the children sleeping during the flight?
Would she fly first class if she had the money?
Will they be traveling in business class?

If the verb is made of just one word, you have to add a form of *do*. Take a look at the following pairs:

She speaks Russian.
Does she speak Russian?
You always buy tickets online.
Do you always buy tickets online?
He got to the airport three hours before his flight left.
Did he get to the airport three hours before his flight left?

Notice that when you add a form of *do*, the main verb goes back to its basic, or infinitive, form. So, in the first pair, *she speaks* becomes *does she speak*, and in the third pair, *he got* becomes *did he get*.

PRACTICE: FORMING QUESTIONS

Now let's practice forming questions. Take a look at each of the statements below, and form the corresponding question. For example, if the statement is: *He goes to the office every morning at 8:30*, then you would form the question: *Does he go to the office every morning at 8:30?*

1. He is taking a taxi to the airport.
2. The immigration official is looking at his passport.
3. He took an earlier flight from Amsterdam.
4. Mrs. Sato will be flying in from Tokyo tomorrow.
5. John uses his cell phone a lot.
6. She bought a new laptop on sale.
7. We speak Japanese at home.
8. The passengers are going through security.
9. They live in a small town far away from the city.
10. Joyce and Harry came here last night.
11. Mr. Thabo lives in South Africa.
12. The kids are learning how to speak Arabic.
13. You sent the letter this morning.
14. The students were listening to the professor.
15. The plane will leave from Gate 28-B.
16. The pilot has just arrived.

STRESS IN QUESTIONS

Now listen to the following four questions and notice the change in stress in the speaker's voice.

🎧 *We will be arriving in New York in **ten minutes**?*
*We will be arriving in **New York** in ten minutes?*
*We will be **arriving** in New York in ten minutes?*
***We** will be arriving in New York in ten minutes?*

📖 Notice that the speaker can specify which information he or she is asking for by stressing a certain word or phrase in the question.

VERBS ENDING IN -*ING*

Throughout this course we'll take time to review several verb tenses that you may need to practice. We'll do that slowly and carefully, and by the end of the course you'll have reviewed all of the major (and most difficult!) tenses that you use in English. For now, let's start with a review of -*ing* verb forms. Take a look at these examples:

The plane is taking off right now.
The flight attendant was walking down the aisle when we hit turbulence.
I will be sleeping when they serve the meal.
We will be landing in a just a few minutes.

Technically, these are called continuous or progressive tenses, and you use them when you want to talk about something that is happening right now, or something that was happening or will be happening over a period of time. It's simple to form them. Just use the right form of *to be* (*am, are, is, was, were, will be*) and then the verb in its *-ing* form. Compare:

Mrs. Tang speaks English. (In general.)
Mrs. Tang is speaking English. (Right now, but perhaps she can also speak Chinese.)
I ate dinner last night at 7:30. (Just a statement about the past.)
I was eating dinner when the phone rang. (My dinner was interrupted by the phone.)
I was eating dinner last night at 7:30. (When 7:30 came around, I had already started but had not yet finished my dinner.)
John reads at the library. (In general. But maybe he's home right now.)
John is reading at the library. (Right now he's at the library.)

You also may have noticed that the *will be . . . -ing* form is used to talk about a plan, or something you're very certain about in the future.

The plane will be landing in fifteen minutes.
We will be eating very soon.
Don't buy that computer today; it will be going on sale next week.

PRACTICE: VERBS ENDING IN *-ING*
Fill in the blanks in each of the following sentences using the verb in parentheses in past progressive, present progressive, or future progressive tense.

1. The pilot _____ _____ an announcement now. (make)
2. The pilot _____ _____ an announcement when we hit turbulence. (make)
3. _____ they _____ Spanish or Portuguese right now? (speak)
4. I _____ _____ _____ a new car next month. (buy)
5. _____ you _____ right now, or can you join me for lunch? (work)
6. _____ we _____ _____ through passport control after we land? (go)
7. The flight attendant _____ _____ _____ beverages very soon. (serve)
8. We _____ _____ through security when the plane took off. (go)
9. Who _____ _____ all of the noise while we _____ _____ last night? (make, sleep)
10. I _____ _____ for a test now; can I call you back? (study)
11. The students _____ _____ excited about summer vacation—it's very soon. (get)
12. What _____ you _____ ? Do you want to come to lunch with me? (do)

1D LISTENING EXERCISE

Listen to the recorded sentences and the question-word clues given. Then form questions with those clues in the pauses provided. For example, if you hear: *Mr. Thabo is standing at the ticket counter. (who?)* You'd form this question: *Who is standing at the ticket counter?* You'll hear the correct answer after each pause.

1. *I'll be staying in the United States for two months.* (how long?)
2. *Collision insurance is included.* (what?)
3. *He'll stay with his sister and her family.* (intonation.)
4. *You can return your car to any of our branches.* (where?)

ANSWER KEY—PRACTICE SECTIONS

VOCABULARY

1. compact	5. dairy	9. unlimited	13. all set
2. prior to	6. window seat	10. drop...off	14. Proceed
3. mandatory	7. aisle	11. included	15. immigration forms
4. branch	8. available	12. smoking section	

QUESTION WORDS

1. Who	5. many	9. which	13. Where
2. Why	6. Where	10. why	14. much
3. When	7. What	11. when	15. How
4. How	8. where	12. Who	

FORMING QUESTIONS

1. Is he taking a taxi to the airport?
2. Is the immigration official looking at his passport?
3. Did he take an earlier flight from Amsterdam?
4. Will Mrs. Sato be flying in from Tokyo tomorrow?
5. Does John use his cell phone a lot?
6. Did she buy a new laptop on sale?
7. Do we speak Japanese at home?
8. Are the passengers going through security?
9. Do they live in a small town far away from the city?
10. Did Joyce and Harry come here last night?
11. Does Mr. Thabo live in South Africa?
12. Are the kids learning how to speak Arabic?
13. Did you send the letter this morning?
14. Were the students listening to the professor?
15. Will the plane leave from Gate 28-B?
16. Has the pilot just arrived?

VERBS WITH -ING

1. is making	5. Are...working	9. ...was making	
2. was making	6. Will...be going	10. am studying	
3. Are...speaking	7. will be serving	11. are getting	
4. will be buying	8. were going	12. are...doing	

LISTENING EXERCISE

1. How long will you be staying in the United States?
2. What is included?
3. He'll stay with his sister and her family?
4. Where can I return the car?

Lesson 2

ASKING FOR DIRECTIONS

In Lesson 2 you'll hear a dialogue about Richard, who is trying to find his way to the center of Stamford. You'll also hear a dialogue about Andrea and Bernard, who are trying to find parking in an unfamiliar town. As you can guess, you'll learn vocabulary and expressions that are useful for driving and asking directions. You'll also review some important expressions with common verbs. Finally, you'll practice commands.

2A DIALOGUE

DIALOGUE 1: CAN YOU TELL ME HOW TO GET TO . . .?

Richard is driving toward Stamford, Connecticut, but he's not familiar with the city and he decides to stop on his way to buy a map. He stops at a convenience store to see if they can help him. Let's listen.

Richard:	*Do you sell maps?*
Salesperson:	*No, I'm sorry, we don't.*
Richard:	*Just my luck.*
Salesperson:	*Maybe I can help you.*
Richard:	*Well, can you tell me how to get to Stamford?*
Salesperson:	*Sure. Follow the highway south for about ten miles, and get off at Exit 30. At the end of the ramp, make a left on to Park Street.*
Richard:	*Left at the end of the ramp?*
Salesperson:	*Yes. Then, at the traffic light, turn right on to Maple Lane. At the next intersection, turn left and you'll be in the center of Stamford.*
Richard:	*Thanks a lot.*
Salesperson:	*You're welcome.*

Now listen to the dialogue again. This time, repeat after the native speakers in the pauses provided.

DIALOGUE 2: NO PARKING!

Andrea and Bernard are in town to run a few errands. The only problem is that they can't find a place to park. They've been driving around looking for parking on the street, but finally they give up and decide to park in a lot. Andrea decides to ask the parking attendant for directions.

Andrea:	*You can't park here! You'll get a ticket!*
Bernard:	*I've had it! Parking in this city is no picnic. Let's look for a parking lot.*
Andrea:	*There's one right over there, and it's only two dollars an hour.*
Attendant:	*Hi. Here's your ticket. Back up in that space next to the blue Honda. Just leave the keys in the car, but remember that we're not responsible for any valuables left in your car.*
Andrea:	*In that case, I'll take my bag with me. By the way, could you tell us how to get to the town hall?*
Attendant:	*No problem. Walk two blocks east on Barrow Street, then make a right. You'll see a gas station on your left. Pass the gas station and make another left down Thompson Street. The town hall will be right in front of you.*
Andrea:	*So, I take a left after the gas station, on to what street?*

Attendant: *Thompson Street.*
Andrea: *Thompson. Thanks.*
Attendant: *Any time.*

Listen to the dialogue a second time, and repeat in the pauses provided.

2B WORDS IN ACTION

Let's go back and review some of the vocabulary that you heard in the dialogues. Remember that you can hear the words and expressions in bold on your recordings to practice your pronunciation. But first, read through all of the vocabulary and practice aloud.

highway (freeway)
A highway (freeway) is a main road with many lanes.

about
The book is about a family's troubles during the Civil War.
You'll be in the car for about two hours.

get off
We'll be getting off the highway in about five minutes. Then we can stop at a gas station.
We'll be getting off the train in two stops.

ramp
To get on or off a highway, you have to take a ramp.
There's a wheelchair ramp that leads to the front door of the library.

traffic
Traffic is very bad at 5:30; everyone is leaving work and trying to get home.

rush hour
It's rush hour at 5:30! Everyone is on the roads.

traffic light
When the traffic light turns green, you can go.

accident
The weather was very bad, and two cars had an accident.
Was anyone hurt in the accident?

speeding
Speeding is illegal! You shouldn't drive faster than the speed limit.
He was speeding, going 80 miles per hour in a 60 mile per hour zone.

exit
At which exit should we get off the highway?

interstate
Route 80 is a big interstate highway; it's a highway that goes through many states.

intersection
You have to watch for traffic if you cross an intersection.

side road
After the snow storm they plowed all of the main roads, but the side roads were still covered.

responsible
You can't count on him! He's not responsible.
Mr. and Mrs. Cranford are looking for a responsible babysitter for their children.
The parking lot is not responsible if something is stolen from your car.

back road
They live on a back road— it's far away from the center of town, in the middle of a forest.

crosswalk
In a crosswalk, pedestrians have the right of way.

valuables
You should lock your passport and any other valuables in the hotel safe.
Don't leave valuables unattended, or they'll be stolen.

stop sign
You always have to stop at a stop sign.

ticket
You'll get a ticket if you park in a no-parking zone.
Don't lose your ticket. Without it, you won't get your car back.

landmark
When you give directions, you should use landmarks, such as gas stations, schools, or churches.

🎧 Now turn on the recording and listen to the vocabulary in bold. Repeat each word or expression, and the example sentence, in the pauses provided.

PRACTICE: VOCABULARY
📖 Now let's practice the vocabulary.

about	crosswalk	interstate
get off	valuables	side road
ramp	stop sign	back road
highway	ticket	traffic
traffic light	accident	rush hour
intersection	speeding	landmark
responsible	exit	

1. Walk up to the _____ if you want to cross the street.
2. Don't drive so quickly! This is a back road, not a _____!

3. I saw a terrible _____ on my way to work this morning. I think people were hurt.

4. The police pulled Rick over for _____; he was driving too fast.

5. The _____ _____ is yellow. Slow down!

6. We're only _____ five or ten minutes from town.

7. Not all teen-agers are _____ enough to take care of a car.

8. Get off the highway at _____ 27B.

9. To go from New Jersey to Ohio you'll need to take an _____ highway.

10. The Morgan's don't live on a main road, but on a _____ _____ with a lot of houses and trees.

11. Don't go home on the highway; take a more interesting route on a _____ _____ so you can see the countryside.

12. The exit _____ for Springfield is five miles up the highway.

13. Drop me off at the _____ of First Avenue and 10th Street.

14. He was driving 80 miles per hour, so of course he got a _____.

15. It took me a long time to get to work this morning because _____ was so heavy.

16. We should wait until after _____ _____ to leave.

17. Don't drive through the _____ _____!

18. You can _____ _____ the subway at Union Square or at Astor Place.

19. The thieves took all of the _____ they could find.

20. Can you tell me what _____ I should look for so I know when to turn off the main road?

2C TAKE A CLOSER LOOK

Now let's go back and review some of the structures and idioms you came across in the dialogues.

EXPRESSIONS WITH COMMON VERBS

In English, there are a lot of important expressions that use common verbs. For example, you probably know that the verb *get* can be used in many different ways. In the two dialogues from this lesson you saw: to get (a ticket), to get to (Stamford), to get off (at Exit 30).

Let's take a closer look at some different expressions formed with a few common verbs. Pay careful attention to the preposition in each example if there is one.

to get
He got a letter from an old friend.
You have to buy a ticket before you get on the train.
We're going to get off the subway at the next stop, so get ready.
How do I get to the Anderson Theater?

I get up every morning at 6:30 and go running before breakfast.
He's moving to Seoul next year, so if he wants to get by he'll need to learn Korean.

to turn
He turned red with anger.
At the intersection, turn on to Main Street.
Turn on the lights so I can see what I'm doing!
Turn off the music; it's too loud!
Can you turn up the volume on the TV? I can't hear what the reporter is saying.
In fairy tales, people often turn into monsters.
The parking lot was full, so the attendant turned us away.
We turned down the wrong road and got lost.
Turn back! This is the wrong way.
You cooked for a lot of people last night! How did the meal turn out?
Bad breath turns me off—I'd never date a guy who didn't use mouthwash.

to look
You look beautiful tonight.
Don't look at me like that!
I don't like your glasses at all. You look like an owl in them!
Dennis looks up to his older brother—he really idolizes him.
Samantha looks down on her colleagues. She thinks she's better than they are.
Could you look over this report and let me know what you think?
I've been looking for my glasses, but I can't find them.
Could you look after my cat while I'm on vacation?

to take
I'll take my bag with me.
If you're hot, take off your coat.
Let's take a trip this spring. I want to go to the Caribbean.
I don't believe what you're saying. Do you take me for a fool?
Don't drive so fast! Take it easy on these curves—it's raining heavily!
I take it back; I shouldn't have said that.
He doesn't look like his mother; he takes after his father.

to go
The alarm went off, and five minutes later the police arrived.
I'm very thirsty. I could really go for a cold drink.
Kevin and Jenny are going out—they've been boyfriend and girlfriend for two months.
The lights are going out all over town—there must be a blackout.
We're lost! Now we're just going around in circles—we've been on this road already!
She's going on and on about her children. She talks too much about them!

Every time I use my cell phone my bill goes up.
The temperature usually goes down at night.
If you take some aspirin, your fever will go down.

to back up
Please back up your car in the corner over there.
I really need your support. Could you back me up on this?
You should back up your files on a diskette so that you have a copy.

🎧 Now turn on the CD and listen to the examples in bold. Repeat in the pauses provided.

PRACTICE: EXPRESSIONS WITH COMMON VERBS

📖 Let's practice some of these expressions. Fill in the blanks using one of the choices provided.

1. Can you tell me how to get _____ (on/off/to) the post office?
2. Could you please turn _____ (up/down/on) the music? It's too loud.
3. That car looks _____ (like/to/after) a beetle.
4. Take _____ (on/after/off) your coat and stay awhile!
5. My alarm clock must be broken; it didn't go _____. (up/off/on)
6. The woman got _____ (on/in/off) the bus and paid her fare.
7. Turn _____ (in/on/off) to Main Street here.
8. The babysitter is looking _____ (at/up/after) the children while their parents go to the movies.
9. Scott was sorry and took _____ (back/after/in) everything he said.
10. Prices go _____ (after/up/through) every year.
11. I think we've turned _____ (back/away/down) the wrong street.
12. Who do you look _____ to? (down/up/at)
13. Could you do me a favor and look _____ (down/in/over) this letter?
14. Take it ____! (in/easy/over) You shouldn't eat so fast!
15. I'm hungry. I could go _____ (for/in/to) something to eat.

COMMANDS

When you ask someone for directions, you're going to hear a lot of commands—*go, turn, stop, continue,* etc. Let's review a few examples of commands.

Turn right at the next traffic light. Don't turn left.
Drive on the right side of the road in the U.S. Don't drive on the left side.
Drop me off at the next corner. Don't drop me off at this corner.
Ask the police officer for directions. Don't ask me.

As you know, the command form of the verb is just its basic form without any endings. And to make a negative command, just add *don't* before the verb.

ARTICLES *A, AN, THE, SOME*

The words *a, an, the,* and *some* are called "articles." You can think
of them as articles of clothing that you use to dress up nouns for
certain occasions. Let's review when to use them, and when not to
use them.

A and *an* are called "indefinite articles." You use them when you're
making a general statement about singular (one item) nouns that you
can count:

A rose is red.
A lion is a dangerous animal.
An umbrella is a good thing to carry when it's raining.
A doctor has to study for many years.

You also use *a* or *an* when you're talking about a non-specific noun or one
that you haven't talked about in the conversation already:

Sherry ate an apple. (Any apple—it's not important to be specific.)
We bought a car last week. (I'll tell you more about the car now...)
Could I borrow a pen from you? (Any pen—it doesn't matter which one.)
This man needs to see a doctor! (Any doctor.)

The is called a "definite article." As you can guess, you use it when you're
talking about a specific noun or specific nouns.

The White House is in Washington, DC.
The milk you put in your coffee is sour.
The woman in the red dress asked Larry on a date.
The first page of the article is very interesting.

You should also use *the* in a conversation when you've already introduced
or mentioned a general noun. The first time you mention it, you should
use *a* or *an*:

We looked at an apartment yesterday. The apartment we looked at was
beautiful.
A dog bit me! My neighbor was walking the dog, and it ran up to me, and...
Don saw a doctor last week. He asked the doctor which medication he
should take.

Some is the plural form of *a* or *an* when you're talking about non-specific
nouns or ones that you haven't talked about in the conversation already:

Sherry ate some apples.
We bought some books last week.
Could I borrow some pens from you?
Some people came to see you while you were out.

But *some* is also used with singular, non-specific nouns that you can't count:

Could I have some tea?
The girl put some water in the bucket.
Kevin always eats some fruit before he goes to work.
I put some sugar in your coffee.

If you're making a general statement about plural nouns that you can count, don't use any article at all:

Roses are red.
Lions are dangerous animals.
Umbrellas are good things to carry when it's raining.
Doctors have to study for many years.

Or, if you're making a general statement about any noun that you cannot count, don't use any article at all:

Fruit is a healthy snack.
Water covers most of the Earth.
Fire is a hazard.
Sugar can give you cavities.

PRACTICE: *A, AN, THE,* AND *SOME*
Complete each of the following sentences with *a, an, the, some,* or no article at all.

1. _____ cactus is a plant that lives with little water.
2. _____ people need to drink _____ water in order to survive.
3. Do you have _____ piece of paper I could use?
4. Do you have _____ piece of paper I gave you yesterday?
5. Dan forgot to bring back _____ umbrella he borrowed.
6. Would you like _____ milk in your tea?
7. _____ gold is a very valuable metal.
8. _____ teacher has to be patient.
9. _____ teachers have to be patient.
10. _____ window is made of _____ glass.
11. I bought _____ new laptop the other week.
12. _____ first month of _____ year is January.
13. Have you ever seen _____ tornado?
14. We rented _____ car and drove to _____ hotel that you recommended.
15. Manhattan is _____ island.
16. _____ basketball players are usually tall.
17. We went to see _____ opera last night. _____ opera we saw was Turandot.
18. Sandy ate _____ orange for breakfast.
19. _____ orange is a good source of vitamin C.
20. There are _____ oranges in the bowl next to the fridge.

2D LISTENING EXERCISE

LISTENING EXERCISE 1

🎧 Listen to the recorded commands and the clues given after each one. Then form new commands with those clues in the pauses provided. For example, if you hear: *Turn left onto Maple Avenue. (Center Street)* You'd form this new command: *Turn left onto Center Street.* You'll hear the correct answer after each pause.

1. *Drive over the bridge.* (around the traffic circle)
2. *Don't park in front of the driveway.* (in a no-parking zone)
3. *Don't park in front of the driveway.* (next to a fire hydrant)
4. *The town hall will be on your right.* (gas station)
5. *The town hall will be on your right.* (the post office)

LISTENING EXERCISE 2

Now listen to the sentences, and then restate them using one of the expressions you learned in this lesson.

1. *I am searching for Thompson Street.*
2. *Of course I will support you.*
3. *My mother takes care of my daughter when I'm gone.*
4. *He looks like my grandmother.*

ANSWER KEY—PRACTICE SECTIONS

VOCABULARY

1. crosswalk
2. highway
3. accident
4. speeding
5. traffic light
6. about
7. responsible
8. exit
9. interstate
10. side road
11. back road
12. ramp
13. intersection
14. ticket
15. traffic
16. rush hour
17. stop sign
18. get off
19. valuables
20. landmark

EXPRESSIONS WITH COMMON VERBS

1. to
2. down
3. like
4. off
5. off
6. on
7. on
8. after
9. back
10. up
11. down
12. up
13. over
14. easy
15. for

A, AN, THE, AND SOME

1. A
2. —/—
3. a
4. the
5. the
6. some
7. —
8. A
9. —
10. A/—
11. a
12. The/the
13. a
14. a/the
15. an
16. —
17. an/The
18. an
19. An
20. some

LISTENING EXERCISE 1

1. Drive around the traffic circle.
2. Don't park in a no-parking zone.
3. Don't park next to a fire hydrant.
4. The gas station will be on your right.
5. The post office will be on your right.

LISTENING EXERCISE 2

1. I'm looking for Thompson Street.
2. Of course I will back you up!
3. My mother looks after my daughter when I'm gone.
4. He takes after my grandmother.

Lesson 3
APARTMENT HUNTING

In this lesson you'll listen in as Steve and Patricia take a look at an apartment they're considering renting. You'll hear a lot of vocabulary associated with living spaces and, of course, practical vocabulary and expressions used by anyone looking for a new place to live. You'll also review personal pronouns and the demonstratives *this*, *that*, *these*, and *those*.

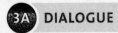

DIALOGUE

WE'LL TAKE IT!

Steve and Patricia are interested in moving into a new apartment. Mr. Berger, a landlord, is showing them one of his apartments available to rent. Let's listen as he takes them through the apartment and answers their questions. First, listen to the dialogue at normal conversational speed.

Mr. Berger:	*Come on in, let me show you around. Here's the living room.*
Patricia:	*Great! The view from this window is wonderful.*
Mr. Berger:	*This is the kitchen.*
Steve:	*It looks new.*
Mr. Berger:	*Yes, we renovated just last year and replaced all the appliances.*
Patricia:	*Just look at all the closet space in the master bedroom!*
Steve:	*Well, I'm sure you can fill those closets in no time.*
Patricia:	*Oh, come on, give me a break. I don't have that much stuff.*
Mr. Berger:	*And here's the bathroom.*
Steve:	*What did you say the rent was?*
Mr. Berger:	*Thirteen hundred dollars a month.*
Patricia:	*Does that include utilities?*
Mr. Berger:	*It includes heat, gas, and hot water. Electricity and telephone are extra.*
Patricia:	*When will the apartment be available?*
Mr. Berger:	*On the first of the month.*
Steve:	*We like it a lot, but we'll have to think about it. Can we call you tomorrow?*
Mr. Berger:	*Sure.*
	(THE NEXT DAY)
Steve:	*Hello, Mr. Berger, this is Steve Heller. I'm calling about the apartment we looked at yesterday. We'd like to take it if it's still available.*
Mr. Berger:	*Great!*
Steve:	*So, what's the next step?*
Mr. Berger:	*I'll draw up a lease and send it to you. What I'll need from you is one month's rent as security deposit, and the first month's rent in advance.*
Steve:	*I'll get the deposit back, won't I?*
Mr. Berger:	*Of course, as long as the place is not damaged beyond the usual wear and tear when you move out.*
Steve:	*Great! Can I send you a check?*
Mr. Berger:	*Sure, a check will be fine. Just send it along with the lease after you've signed it.*
Steve:	*Thanks!*

Now listen to the dialogue again, and repeat after the native speakers in the pauses.

3B WORDS IN ACTION

Let's see some vocabulary in action. Remember that you can hear the words and expressions in bold on your recordings, but first read through all of the vocabulary and practice aloud.

ad
*Did you see any **ads** for two-bedroom apartments in the paper?*

classifieds
*I saw the ad in the **classifieds**.*

available
*Is the apartment still **available**, or has someone else taken it?*

renovated
When we bought the apartment, it was in terrible condition. But we recently renovated it, so now everything is new.

landlord
*The **landlord** owns the apartment.*

tenant
*The **tenant** rents the apartment.*

appliance
The appliances are all new; we just bought a stove, refrigerator, and dishwasher.

master
Jason is a master chess player. No one can beat him.
These are the master controls; they control everything.
If you practice enough, you can master any language.

storage space
*Is there **storage space** in the building where I can keep my bike?*

laundry room
*You can wash your clothes in the **laundry room** in the basement.*

lease
*You should read the **lease** carefully before you sign it.*

deposit
You have to leave a deposit if you want to rent a bike.
Please deposit a quarter to continue this game.

in advance
Professor Jackman's exams are always easy because she gives us the questions in advance.

the usual wear and tear
A few stains on the carpet? That's the usual wear and tear.

🎧 Now turn on the recordings and listen to the vocabulary in bold. Repeat each word or expression, and the example sentence, in the pauses provided.

PRACTICE: VOCABULARY

📖 Now let's practice that vocabulary.

ad	appliances	lease
classifieds	tenant	deposit
available	masters	in advance
renovated	storage space	the usual wear and
landlord	laundry room	tear

1. Seth has been in the _____ _____ for hours; he's got a lot of clothes to wash.
2. I need to buy a toaster. Where can I get small kitchen _____?
3. After people saw the _____ in the newspaper, the restaurant was full every night.
4. If she's late again on her rent, she's going to have a problem with the _____.
5. Judy and Peter's dog did so much damage to the apartment that the landlord kept all of their security _____.
6. A car that old is going to have _____ _____ _____ _____ _____.
7. We're going to rent a _____ _____ to keep our bikes, winter clothes, and other things we don't need all the time.
8. Sally needs to find a cheap used car, so she's looking through the _____.
9. Sasha is a good dancer because he practices and practices until he _____ every move.
10. The landlord just sent me my copy of the _____, signed by both of us.
11. Rita was always a very good _____; she never made noise and she paid the rent on time every month.
12. The Freids are moving out the end of March, so their apartment will be _____ on April 1.
13. These cabinets are so old, it looks like they haven't been _____ in thirty years!
14. He signed the lease without even seeing the apartment _____ _____? That's crazy!

3C TAKE A CLOSER LOOK

Now let's stop and take a closer look at some of the structures used in the dialogue.

CONTRACTIONS, PART 1

In the dialogue, you heard Steve say to Mr. Berger, *"I'm calling about the apartment we looked at yesterday."* As you know, it's more natural for people to say *I'm* instead of *I am*, or *she's* instead of *she is*. Let's practice some of these shortened forms, or contractions.

🎧 *I'm the owner of this building.*
You're the new tenant in 202?
The check's in the mail.
They've decided to take the apartment.
We'll be back in a minute.
He'd like to discuss this with his wife first.
She's in the basement.
He's been living here for a long time.

📖 As you can see, you can form contractions with: *am, are, is, will, have, has, had, would.*

I am your new neighbor.	*I'm your new neighbor.*
They are making too much noise!	*They're making too much noise!*
She is always complaining about us.	*She's always complaining about us.*
We will have to move next month.	*We'll have to move next month.*
I have been at the office all day.	*I've been at the office all day.*
He has never lived in such a big house.	*He's never lived in such a big house.*
They had already packed their things.	*They'd already packed their things.*
We would never live here!	*We'd never live here!*

PRACTICE: CONTRACTIONS, PART 1

Re-write each of the following sentences using contractions.

1. She is the best landlord in town.
2. They had only seen the apartment once.
3. I will send you the lease tomorrow.
4. You would complain if you lived here, too!
5. The landlords said they are keeping the deposit.
6. He will send a security deposit with the first month's rent.
7. I have never seen such a filthy apartment!
8. Gordon is coming over to speak to her.
9. They would rather live in a house.
10. You will sign this lease tomorrow.

PERSONAL PRONOUNS

Now look back for a moment at the examples of contractions you saw. Read the first words of each sentence: *I'm, you're, he'd*, etc. Let's take another look at how these subject pronouns are used in sentences.

I'm looking for a new apartment.	
You have to move next month.	
Mr. Berger is my landlord.	*He's my landlord.*
Patricia is my neighbor.	*She's my neighbor.*
The building is new.	*It's new.*
Amanda and I haven't signed the lease yet.	*We haven't signed the lease yet.*
David and George are in the hall.	*They're in the hall.*

Don't forget that object pronouns can be different from subject pronouns. Here are some examples:

I am watching TV.	but	*You are watching **me**.*
He is speaking.	but	*I am speaking to **him**.*
She understands.	but	*He understands **her**.*
We're looking at it.	but	*The landlord's showing **us** around.*
They can't move yet.	but	*Have you seen **them** yet?*

Remember that *you* and *it* never change: ***You** see me, and I see **you**. **It's** a new building; have you seen **it**?*

PRACTICE: PERSONAL PRONOUNS

Complete each of the following with one of the choices given.

1.   _____ (I/Me) am excited about moving.
2.   The apartment isn't big enough for _____ (we/us), so we won't take _____ (it/them).
3.   The landlord is on the phone. _____ (She/Her) wants to speak to you.
4.   Could you give _____ (they/them) a message for _____ (I/me)?
5.   Did you understand what ____ (he/him) said? I can't understand _____ (he/him).
6.   Give _____ (she/her) a call in the morning.
7.   _____ (They/Them) will be moving in next to _____ (we/us).
8.   _____ (I/Me) can't speak to John right now. Tell _____ (he/him) that ____ (I/me) will call ____ (he/him) later.
9.   Mary knows the Garcias. ____ (He/She) lives in the same building as _____ (they/them) do.
10. Joyce is my boss. _____ (I/Me) work for _____ (she/her).

THIS, THAT, THESE, THOSE

In the dialogue, Patricia says, *"The view from this window is wonderful!"*
The word *this* is called a demonstrative—it's used to point to a particular
thing. The demonstratives in English are: *this, that, these,* and *those.*

Remember that *this* is used to point to a singular thing (one window, in
Patricia's example) that's close to the speaker. *That* is used to point to a
singular thing that's far from the speaker. *These* is used to point to more
than one thing close to the speaker, and *those* is used to point to more
than one thing far from the speaker. They are sometimes used with
expressions such as *over there* or *here*, but more often you can guess the
position of the item by which demonstrative is used, so these words
aren't needed. Let's look at some examples:

This new book I'm reading is very interesting.
That building over there is where I work.
These windows are really dirty and need to be cleaned!
Those people walking on the other side of the street look familiar.

In the examples above, *this, that, these,* and *those* all come right before
the noun they are "demonstrating": *book, building, windows, people.* But
you can also use them as pronouns, just like *I, you, he, it,* etc.

This is the best apartment I've ever had!
Did you hear that?
I hate those shoes! I'd rather wear these.
Those are the two most popular restaurants in town.

PRACTICE: THIS, THAT, THESE, THOSE

Complete each of the following sentences with *this, that, these,* or *those.*

1. Have you had a chance to read _____ report I'm holding?
2. _____ women over there work in my department.
3. I want to take _____ one here.
4. _____ songs we're listening to are not very good!
5. I really like _____ songs we heard yesterday at the concert.
6. Can you see _____ plane way up in the sky?
7. Who are _____ people standing over by the door?
8. _____ house we're in front of is mine.
9. Whose coins are _____, the ones I'm holding?
10. Look over there! What on earth is _____?

3D LISTENING EXERCISE

Listen to the recorded questions. Answer each one in the affirmative—with "yes"—and use a contraction in your answer. For example, if you hear *"Will he move next month?"* you should answer, *"Yes, he'll move next month."*

1. *Will she take the apartment?*
2. *Are they moving in tomorrow?*
3. *Would you like to think about it?*
4. *Has he signed the lease yet?*
5. *Is she sending a check?*
6. *Are you going to paint the bedroom?*
7. *Have we talked about this already?*

ANSWER KEY—PRACTICE SECTIONS

VOCABULARY
1. laundry room
2. appliances
3. ad
4. landlord
5. deposit
6. the usual wear and tear
7. storage space
8. classifieds
9. masters
10. lease
11. tenant
12. available
13. renovated
14. in advance

CONTRACTIONS, PART 1
1. She's the best landlord in town.
2. They'd only seen the apartment once.
3. I'll send you the lease tomorrow.
4. You'd complain if you lived here, too!
5. The landlords said they're keeping the deposit.
6. He'll send a security deposit with the first month's rent.
7. I've never seen such a filthy apartment.
8. Gordon's coming over to speak to her.
9. They'd rather live in a house.
10. You'll sign this lease tomorrow.

PERSONAL PRONOUNS
1. I
2. us, it
3. She
4. them, me
5. he, him
6. her
7. They, us
8. I, him, I, him
9. She, they
10. I, her

THIS, THAT, THESE, THOSE
1. this
2. Those
3. this
4. These
5. those
6. that
7. those
8. This
9. these
10. that

LISTENING EXERCISE
1. Yes, she'll take the apartment
2. Yes, they're moving in tomorrow.
3. Yes, I'd like to think about it.
4. Yes, he's signed the lease.
5. Yes, she's sending a check.
6. Yes, I'm going to paint the bedroom.
7. Yes, we've talked about this already.

Lesson 4

GETTING THINGS FIXED

In Lesson 4 you'll listen to a dialogue between Mario and his landlord, Mr. Watson. Mario tells his landlord about several things that need to be fixed in his apartment, so you'll learn a lot of vocabulary that deals with household repairs. Then you'll review more contractions, expressions of quantity, and, finally, how and when to use the simple present tense and the present continuous tense. As always, move at your own pace and listen to the recording as many times as you need.

4A DIALOGUE

A FEW PROBLEMS

Mario has just moved into a new apartment, and he's found some things that need to be fixed. Let's listen in as he calls Mr. Watson, his landlord, to tell him about these problems.

Mario:	*Mr. Watson, this is Mario, your tenant in 6B.*
Mr. Watson:	*Hi. What's up?*
Mario:	*There are a few problems with the apartment. First, the faucet in the bathtub drips constantly.*
Mr. Watson:	*I'll ask my plumber to come by and fix it tomorrow.*
Mario:	*Also, one of the burners on the stove doesn't work.*
Mr. Watson:	*What's the matter with it?*
Mario:	*I can't control the temperature. I think you'll have to get an electrician.*
Mr. Watson:	*I'll see what I can do. Is that everything?*
Mario:	*Well, there's one more thing. I can't get a dial tone on the phone; it's dead.*
Mr. Watson:	*I'm sorry, there's nothing I can do about that. You'll have to call the phone company.*

Now it's time to listen to the dialogue again and repeat after the native speakers in the pauses provided.

4B WORDS IN ACTION

Let's review some vocabulary that will come in handy if you ever need to have anything repaired. First, read through the entire list aloud and practice.

What's up?
—Hi, John, what's up? —Not much. What's up with you?
Cindy seems to have a problem. Do you know what's up with her?

faucet
Turn on the faucet and see if there's any hot water.

broken
The lock on the front door is broken; the key won't turn.

come by
Come by tomorrow around 3:00.
Mrs. Wong came by my office yesterday and gave me this report.

radiator
The radiators are too hot; I can't control the heat.

burner
There are four burners on the stove, but only three work.

control
We can't control the weather, but we hope it will be sunny.
Could you please control your children? They're disturbing us.

electrician
If something is wrong with your stove, call an electrician.

thermostat
I don't think the thermostat works. It's set at 68 degrees, but it's freezing in here!

plumber
A plumber can fix your toilet.

drain
The drain is at the bottom of the sink.
Turn off the faucet in the bathtub and let the water drain out.

leak
There's a leak in the roof; every time it rains, water comes in through the ceiling.
The faucet is leaking water all day.

clog
The water won't drain from the sink. There must be a clog.

cracked
The kids broke the window— it's cracked.

water heater
There was no hot water again when I took a shower. I think we need a new water heater.

locksmith
You lost your keys and can't get into your apartment? Call a locksmith!

🎧 Now turn on the recordings and listen to the vocabulary in bold. Repeat each word or expression, and the example sentence, in the pauses provided.

PRACTICE: VOCABULARY

📖 Now let's practice all of this new vocabulary. Complete the sentences using each of the words and expressions listed below only once.

what ... up	controls	leaking
faucet	electrician	clog
broken	thermostat	cracked
come by	plumber	water heater
radiator	drain	locksmith
burner		

1. The toilet isn't flushing. There must be a _____.
2. We should call a _____ to fix the toilet.
3. Hey, Rick, _____ was _____ with you yesterday? You seemed upset.
4. The _____ repaired the lock and gave me a new set of keys.
5. You might want to get a new glass; this one is slightly _____.
6. The wires were so old we needed to have an _____ replace them all.
7. I heard the _____ dripping all night long! It must be _____.
8. Don't use that toaster; it's _____.
9. Don't leave anything on top of the _____; it gets very hot.
10. Could you _____ _____ my office later today? I need to speak to you.
11. The landlord finally replaced the _____ _____ after all the tenants complained about cold water.
12. Where's the _____? I want to turn down the heat a bit.
13. Pull the plug and let the water _____ from the sink.
14. The landlord _____ the heat in the entire building.
15. Don't touch the front left _____. It's off, but it's still hot.

4C   TAKE A CLOSER LOOK

Let's go back now and look at some of the structures covered in the dialogue you just read.

CONTRACTIONS, PART 2

In Lesson 3 we reviewed contractions such as *I'm, you're, he's*, etc. Now let's review contractions with the word *not*. First, listen to the recordings.

🎧 *The stove doesn't work.*
I can't call the electrician; I don't have his number.
They weren't able to use the phone.
I wouldn't pay for a broken lock.
I won't be able to fix your phone tomorrow.

📖 Now let's take a look at some pairs of examples. Notice that negative forms of *to be* (*are not, is not, was not*, etc.), as in "*They are not at home today*," can be restated in two different ways with a contraction.

🎧 *They're not at home today.*
They aren't at home today.
We've not been here before.
We haven't been here before.
It isn't fair.
It's not fair.

📖 Except for first person negative: There's only one way to restate *I am not*.

🎧 *I'm not sure how to repair this.*

PRACTICE: CONTRACTIONS, PART 2
📖 Restate each of the following sentences using a contraction. Remember that there may be more than one answer. If so, write both possible answers.

1. I am not going to fix the toilet myself.
2. He cannot call the landlord about the problems until tomorrow.
3. I would not call a locksmith.
4. It is not possible to control the weather.
5. They are not able to repair the wiring themselves.
6. They were not able to find a good electrician.
7. Susan will not take the apartment after all.
8. You cannot find a better tenant!
9. We had not been living there for very long.
10. It is not fair!

SIMPLE PRESENT VS. PRESENT CONTINUOUS
In the dialogue, Mario described his household problems to his landlord, Mr. Watson. Did you notice the verbs that he used? Since he was describing general conditions in his apartment, he used the simple present tense. For example:

*The faucet in the bathtub **drips** constantly.*
*One of the burners on the stove **doesn't work**.*

These are good examples of the simple present tense, which is used to describe general conditions or truths. You may often hear words like always, usually, constantly, normally, or regularly along with this tense. Let's take a look at some more examples:

*Most people in the United States **speak** English.*
*Many commuters **take** the subway each day in New York.*
*The Andes Mountains **stretch** the entire length of South America.*
*I usually **don't wake up** before 7:00 in the morning.*
*My neighbor constantly **listens** to her radio.*
*They normally **don't arrive** until after 9:00.*

In Lesson 1 we reviewed -*ing* verbs, also called progressive or continuous tenses. The present continuous, which is one of the -*ing* tenses, is another option you have to describe something in the present, but instead of a general or usual condition, it describes something that is happening right now, as you speak. In fact, you'll often hear *now* or *right now* with this tense.

*My neighbor **is listening** to her radio right now.*
*Not many commuters **are taking** the subway this morning.*
*They**'re arriving** right now as we speak.*
*I**'m** still **waking** up; I need to have a cup of coffee!*

PRACTICE: SIMPLE PRESENT VS. PRESENT CONTINUOUS

Chose the correct verb form in each of the following sentence. Remember to look for clues that will help you make your choice.

1. They always _____ (go/are going) out to dinner after work.
2. The landlord _____ (fixes/is fixing) the broken faucet right now.
3. The water heater never _____ (works/is working).
4. The president of the company _____ (meets/is meeting) with us every Thursday.
5. I _____ (speak/am speaking)! Could you please pay attention?
6. When _____ (do/are) you _____ (leave/leaving) for work every morning?
7. The Mississippi _____ (runs/is running) through the middle of the U.S.
8. Joan _____ (looks/is looking) for a new computer.
9. The director _____ (writes/is writing) a report that she'll submit to the board.
10. The director _____ (writes/is writing) reports that she submits to the board.

EXPRESSIONS OF QUANTITY

In the dialogue, Mario complained to his landlord that there were a few problems with his apartment. *A few* is just one important quantity expression in English. Let's review the most important ones now.

a few/a little

Use *a few* to talk about things that you can count, such as problems in an apartment. Use *a little* to talk about things that you can't count, such as time or water or trouble.

I take a few lumps of sugar in my coffee.
I take a little sugar in my coffee.
She already has a few dents in her car.
She already has a little trouble with her new car.

fewer/less

Use *fewer* with things you can count and *less* with things you can't.

I have fewer projects to work on than you do.
She has less responsibility than her boss does.
There were fewer nice days this week than last.
There was less rain this week than last.

many/much

Use *many* to talk about things you can count, and *much* to talk about things you can't count.

How many books did you read last month?
How much work did you get done this week?
It seems that there are so many criminals these days!
It seems that there is so much crime these days!

some, a lot of, no, more

You can use these expressions of quantity both with things you can count and with things you can't count.

He bought some new shirts yesterday.
I still have some time left; we can get another cup of coffee.
There are a lot of passengers waiting to get on the plane.
There isn't a lot of money left in our budget.
They have no computers for that price.
There is no meat in that dish; it's vegetarian.
I got more sleep than you did.
I slept more hours than you did.

any

The word *any* is used in two ways: in questions (either positive or negative), and in negative statements. As with *some, a lot of, no,* and *more, any* can be used in expressions of quantity both with things you can count and things you can't count.

Do you have any safety pins?
I don't have any safety pins.
Don't you have any sugar?
No, I don't have any sugar.

Any also replaces *no* when the verb in the sentence is made negative.

They want no help with the project.
They don't want any help with the project.

If you wish to respond to an *any* question with a positive answer, use *some, a lot of, a little,* or *a few,* depending on the nature of your answer.

Are you going to buy any groceries on the way home?
Yes, I'm going to buy some groceries.
Yes, I'm going to buy a lot of groceries.
Yes, I'm going to buy a few groceries.
Do you want any sugar in your coffee?

Yes, I want some sugar in my coffee.
Yes, I want a lot of sugar in my coffee.
Yes, I want a little sugar in my coffee.

Similarly, questions using *some, a lot of, a little,* or *a few* are usually answered using *any* when the answer is absolutely negative.

Do you want some sunscreen?
No, I don't want any (sunscreen).
Did you eat a lot of blueberries at the picnic?
No, I didn't eat any blueberries.
Do you need a little help?
No, I don't need any help.
Can I borrow a few shirts from you?
No, you can't borrow any shirts from me.

PRACTICE: EXPRESSIONS OF QUANTITY
Choose the right expression of quantity for each of the following sentences.

1.   We can't see everything in so _____ (few/little) time.
2.   There weren't _____ (much/many) guests at the party.
3.   I can't buy that—I have _____ (any/no) money left!
4.   It's too sweet! You used too _____ (many/much) sugar.
5.   You must really like music—you have _____ (a lot of/some) CD's.
6.   There were _____ (fewer/less) people at the conference this year.
7.   I'm tired; I have so _____ (few/little) energy today!
8.   This computer has _____ (fewer/less) memory than that one.
9.   There was so _____ (many/much) corruption under their last mayor.
10. We have to go quickly; we don't have _____ (many/much) time.
11. Did you see any ghosts in the haunted house? Yes, we saw _____ (a little, a few).
12. There aren't _____ (no, any) papers on my desk.

4D LISTENING EXERCISE

🎧 Listen to each of the recorded sentences, and rephrase in the negative using a contraction. For example, if you hear, "*I can write the report,*" the answer you should give is "*I can't write the report.*"

1.   *Peter can repair the stove himself.*
2.   *He was at home when I called.*
3.   *It works!*
4.   *They've broken the window.*
5.   *I'm joining you tonight.*

ANSWER KEY—PRACTICE SECTIONS

VOCABULARY

1. clog	5. cracked	9. radiator	13. drain
2. plumber	6. electrician	10. come by	14. controls
3. what . . . up	7. faucet/leaking	11. water heater	15. burner
4. locksmith	8. broken	12. thermostat	

CONTRACTIONS, PART 2

1. I'm not going to fix the toilet myself.
2. He can't call the landlord about the problems until tomorrow.
3. I wouldn't call a locksmith. (I'd not call a locksmith.)
4. It's not possible to control the weather. (It isn't possible to control the weather.)
5. They're not able to repair the wiring themselves. (They aren't able to repair the wiring themselves.)
6. They weren't able to find a good electrician.
7. Susan won't take the apartment after all.
8. You can't find a better tenant!
9. We hadn't been living there for very long. (We'd not been living there for very long.)
10. It's not fair! (It isn't fair!)

SIMPLE PRESENT VS. PRESENT CONTINUOUS

1. go	4. meets	7. runs	9. is writing
2. is fixing	5. am speaking	8. is looking	10. writes
3. works	6. do . . . leave		

EXPRESSIONS OF QUANTITY

1. little	4. much	7. little	10. much
2. many	5. a lot of	8. less	11. a few
3. no	6. fewer	9. much	12. any

LISTENING EXERCISE

1. No, Peter can't repair the stove himself.
2. He wasn't at home when I called.
3. It doesn't work!
4. They haven't broken the window. They've not broken the window.
5. I'm not joining you tonight.

Lesson 5
DAILY HOUSEHOLD CHORES

In Lesson 5 you'll listen to a dialogue between two people discussing household chores. Naturally, you'll learn some vocabulary that will be useful for talking about doing things around the house—the cooking, the cleaning, and other things no one likes but everyone has to do! You'll also learn more about tag questions and how to express the future.

5A DIALOGUE

YOU'LL DO THAT, WON'T YOU?

Megumi and Kenji are at home talking about all of the little things that need to be done around the house. As a couple, they share these responsibilities, but sometimes they have to do a little bargaining with each other. Let's listen in.

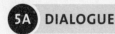

Megumi: *You said you'd do the dishes, didn't you?*
Kenji: *Only if you clear the table.*
Megumi: *C'mon! I made dinner, didn't I?*
Kenji: *Yes, and it was delicious. All right, I'll do the dishes.*
Megumi: *Thanks. And while we're talking about chores, the light in the basement burned out.*
Kenji: *I'll replace the bulb in a minute.*
Megumi: *No, no, I already tried that. It still doesn't work.*
Kenji: *Maybe there's a short. Did you try the fuse box?*
Megumi: *Yes, and that didn't help either.*
Kenji: *Then we should call an electrician, shouldn't we?*
Megumi: *Do you have his number?*
Kenji: *It's on the bulletin board.*
Megumi: *You'll call him tomorrow, won't you?*
Kenji: *Sure, if I remember.*

Now listen to the dialogue again and repeat after the native speakers in the pauses provided.

5B WORDS IN ACTION

Now let's review the vocabulary from the dialogue. First read through the entire list aloud.

do the dishes
I always cook the meal and do the dishes. It's not fair!

clear the table
We're finished with dinner. Let's clear the table so we can do the dishes.

set the table
When you set the table, put the forks on the left and the knife and spoon on the right.

chores
Household chores include cleaning, fixing things, and generally maintaining your home.
I really don't like them at all. It's such a chore to visit them!

tidy up (straighten up)
We should really tidy up/straighten up; the place is a mess and we have guests coming!

burned out (burnt out)
The light is not working; it must have burned out.
Sally is really tired of her job and she's making a lot of mistakes. I think she's burnt out.

short
If you have a short in your electrical system, call an electrician.

fuse
We've lost power—go check the fuse box in the basement.
They were running too many appliances at the same time, and they blew the fuse!
Sam's really got a short fuse. He gets angry very quickly!

bulb
Could you change the bulb in the kitchen lamp, please?

bulletin board
We hang important notes and phone numbers on the bulletin board in our kitchen.
He posted a request for a Spanish teacher on the bulletin board at school.
My Internet chess club has a bulletin board where we post messages.

🎧 Now turn on the recordings and listen to the vocabulary in bold. Repeat each word or expression, and the example sentence, in the pauses provided.

PRACTICE: VOCABULARY

📖 Now it's time to practice the vocabulary.

do the dishes	tidy up (straighten	fuse
clear the table	up)	bulb
set the table	burnt out	bulletin board
chores	short	

1. The lamp fell over and the _____ broke into a thousand pieces.
2. The children do _____ around the house to help their parents.
3. If I rinse and you dry, it'll be much easier to _____ _____ _____.
4. If you need someone to help you around the house, you should post something on the _____ _____.
5. Poor Richard has been working here for too long; I really think he's _____ _____ and should try to find something new.
6. Dinner is going to be ready in five minutes, and we haven't even _____ _____ _____! Let's hurry!
7. Of course the _____ blew! You were running the air conditioner, the dishwasher, and the washing machine all at the same time!

8. We have a lot of trouble with the electrical system in our new home. We just had another _____ this morning.

9. As soon as we _____ _____ _____ we can have dessert in the family room.

10. Wow, your apartment is really a mess! Don't you think you should _____ _____ a bit?

5C TAKE A CLOSER LOOK

Now we'll go back and take a closer look at some of the structures or idioms you heard used in the dialogues.

TAG QUESTIONS

In the first line of the dialogue, Megumi says to Kenji: *"You said you'd do the dishes, didn't you?" "Didn't you?"* is called a tag question. Tag questions are short questions that you can put on the end of a statement you make to ask whether or not it's true. You use them when you're confident that what you're saying is the truth, whether the statement you're making is positive or negative. Let's listen to a few examples of tag questions with positive statements on your recordings.

Ann can cook, can't she?
Peter did the dishes, didn't he?
Roger has called, hasn't he?
You're cold, aren't you?

Notice that in the previous examples, the statement, or first part, of the examples are all positive, but the tag questions are in the negative, with a form of *not*. Now let's look at a few more examples, and this time we'll put the statement in the negative.

Ann can't cook, can she?
Peter didn't do the dishes, did he?
Roger hasn't called, has he?
You're not cold, are you?

With these last four examples, the tag question was positive, because the statement was in the negative.

The tag line is formed by turning the main verb in the sentence into a question, shortening the question to a verb and a subject, and making it negative or positive to contradict the statement.

Ann can cook. → Can she? → Can't she? → Ann can cook, can't she?
Ann can't cook. → Can't she? → Can she? → Ann can't cook, can she?
Roger has called. → Has he? → Hasn't he? → Roger has called, hasn't he?
Roger hasn't called. → Hasn't he? → Has he? → Roger hasn't called, has he?

If you can remember from Lesson 1, many verbs use an auxiliary verb, *do*, when in question form. Look at the following examples:

You went to the store again. → Did you? → Didn't you? → You went to the store again, didn't you?
You speak English. → Do you? → Don't you? → You speak English, don't you?

In these examples, the auxiliary verb *do* is used to form the tag line.

Just remember: question, shorten, and contradict.

If you make a statement with *neither, never, barely, none, nobody*, or *hardly*, you use a positive tag question.

Peter hardly ever does the dishes, does he?
None of your friends liked my cooking, did they?

Let's look at a few more examples:

Neither one of them will come to work, will they?
You've barely even started the report, have you?
You never get to work on time, do you?
None of the applicants will get the job, will they?
None of them can speak Chinese, can they?
Nobody will come to work in such a blizzard, will they?

PRACTICE: TAG QUESTIONS
Complete each of the following with the correct tag question.

1. You work on the eleventh floor, _____ _____?
2. Mr. Richardson takes the train to work, _____ _____?
3. You don't live there, _____ _____?
4. Nobody bought your old computer, _____ _____?
5. She doesn't cook very well, _____ _____?
6. You've hardly even started the work, _____ _____?
7. Nobody is getting a raise this year, _____ _____?
8. They can't understand the instructions, _____ _____?

EXPRESSING THE FUTURE
In the dialogue you saw a few examples of the future tense with *will*. This is the easiest way to express the future, and you can use it when you're speaking about a plan, a promise, or an intention you have.

I promise I will clean the entire apartment this weekend.
I'll do the dishes tonight.
John says that he'll go back to school next year for a Masters.

Will you water my plants while I'm on vacation?
They'll buy new computers for the entire department before the end of the year.

Notice that the usual contraction for *will not* is *won't*.

I won't be home before 8:00 tonight.
She won't be happy when she hears about this!
Won't you be in a meeting tomorrow at 3:00?
Promise me you won't do that again!

Another easy way to express the future is with *going to*. This often sounds less definite than the future with *will*, but the two constructions are very often interchangeable.

He's going to leave for work early tomorrow to beat the traffic.
Mrs. Ang is going to give me the recipe for this dish.
I'm not going to tell you one more time!
Are you going to come back tonight or tomorrow?

You may also hear people expressing the future by using the simple present tense, especially in conversation.

We love traveling—next year we go to Beijing!
I go to the dentist's before work tomorrow.
When do you leave for Amsterdam?
John graduates from college this May.

PRACTICE: EXPRESSING THE FUTURE
Change each of the following sentences into the future using the clues provided. Use contractions where possible.

1. I do the report. (will, tomorrow)
2. She studies at the university this year. (will, next year)
3. They take the bus every day. (going, tonight)
4. Mr. and Mrs. Lee are touring Italy right now. (next month)
5. You have to buy a new computer now. (will, soon)
6. I send you the report by e-mail. (will, tomorrow)
7. John is coming to the party now. (going, later)
8. Sarah is finishing her degree right now. (next spring)
9. Jack does not work today. (will, tomorrow)
10. The director is taking lunch right now. (going, 1:00)
11. I go to the gym on Thursdays. (will, in a few minutes)
12. We see each other every week. (going, next week)

5D LISTENING EXERCISE

🎧 Make tag questions using each of the following statements. For example, if you hear "She's Mexican," you'd say "She's Mexican, isn't she?"

1. *You're hungry.*
2. *No one hurt him.*
3. *He's never enjoyed sports.*
4. *They will help me tonight.*
5. *We can't take the car there.*
6. *Your brother has a cold.*

ANSWER KEY—PRACTICE SECTIONS

VOCABULARY
1. bulb
2. chores
3. do the dishes
4. bulletin board
5. burnt out
6. set the table
7. fuse
8. short
9. clear the table
10. tidy up/ straighten up

TAG QUESTIONS
1. don't you
2. doesn't he
3. do you
4. did they
5. does she
6. have you
7. are they
8. can they

EXPRESSING THE FUTURE
1. I'll do the report tomorrow.
2. She'll study a the university next year.
3. They're going to take the bus tonight.
4. Mr. and Mrs. Lee are touring Italy next month.
5. You'll have to buy a new computer soon.
6. I'll send you the report by e-mail tomorrow.
7. John's going to come to the party later.
8. Sarah finishes her degree next spring.
9. Jack won't work tomorrow.
10. The director is going to take lunch at 1:00.
11. I'll go to the gym in a few minutes.
12. We're going to see each other next week.

LISTENING EXERCISE
1. You're hungry, aren't you?
2. No one hurt him, did they?
3. He's never enjoyed sports, has he?
4. They will help me tonight, won't they?
5. We can't take the car there, can we?
6. Your brother has a cold, doesn't he?

Lesson 6
ALL ABOUT FOOD

As you can probably guess from its name, Lesson 6 will concentrate on food. You'll hear two dialogues, one that deals with planning a dinner and another that deals with ordering a quick lunch. Naturally you'll learn a lot of important vocabulary that you can use every day. You'll also review how to make suggestions and recommendations, and how to use the words *may* and *might*.

6A DIALOGUE

DIALOGUE 1: WHAT'S FOR DINNER TONIGHT?

Richard would like to cook dinner for himself and Sveta, so he asks her what she would like to eat. Let's listen as they share their suggestions and make a shopping list.

Richard:	*I was thinking of cooking dinner tonight. Any ideas?*
Sveta:	*What about roast chicken? Or beef stew?*
Richard:	*I could go for roast chicken.*
Sveta:	*All right. Do we need to get anything?*
Richard:	*I'm making a shopping list right now. What kind of vegetables would you like?*
Sveta:	*How about cabbage and potatoes?*
Richard:	*Sounds good. In that case, let's get a whole chicken, some cabbage, and a bag of potatoes.*
Sveta:	*And what about dessert?*
Richard:	*Why don't we have hot fudge sundaes?*
Sveta:	*Mmm—sounds delicious.*
Richard:	*I don't have much cash left. I'll have to stop by the bank before I go to the supermarket. It might take me a while.*
Sveta:	*Take your time.*

Now listen to the dialogue again. This time, repeat after the native speakers in the pauses provided.

DIALOGUE 2: WHAT CAN I GET YOU?

Of course, not everyone likes to cook, and even if you do like to cook, you don't always have the time. Let's listen while Joan orders a quick lunch on her lunch break.

Salesperson:	*Next.*
Joan:	*I'd like a ham sandwich, please.*
Salesperson:	*What kind of bread?*
Joan:	*Whole wheat.*
Salesperson:	*Mustard or mayonnaise?*
Joan:	*A little mayonnaise, please.*
Salesperson:	*Lettuce and tomato?*
Joan:	*Yes, please.*
Salesperson:	*And how about some cheese?*
Joan:	*I'll take some Swiss, please.*
Salesperson:	*That's ham on whole wheat with Swiss, lettuce and tomato, and a little mayonnaise?*
Joan:	*That's right.*

Listen to the dialogue a second time, and repeat in the pauses provided.

6B WORDS IN ACTION

 idea
I have a great idea for a gift for Mom. Do you want to hear what it is?
I have no idea what 34,784,887 divided by 13,576 is.

shopping list
Don't forget to put juice on your shopping list.

aisle
—Which aisle are cereals in? —Aisle five.

half a pound of roast beef
If I get half a pound of roast beef, I should be able to make sandwiches for all of us.

a loaf of white bread
A loaf of white bread should last three or four days.

a stick of butter
The recipe calls for an entire stick of butter.

a bowl of chicken soup
I'm not all that hungry; a bowl of chicken soup will do.

a can of beans
A can of beans is not expensive.

a box of cereal
A box of cereal shouldn't cost more than three dollars!

a bottle of Coke
I'm thirsty; can you get me a bottle of Coke?

dairy
Milk, yogurt, and cheese are all dairy products.

a carton of orange juice
The kids can drink a whole carton of orange juice in a day!

a dozen
A carton holds a dozen eggs.

container
Fresh olives come in a small plastic container.

🎧 Now turn on the recordings and listen to the vocabulary in bold. Repeat each word or expression, and the example sentence, in the pauses provided.

PRACTICE: VOCABULARY

📖 Are you familiar with all of the vocabulary from this lesson? If not, go back and listen again. If you're ready to practice what you've learned, fill in the blanks in each of the following sentences using the words and expressions listed below. Each one will only be used once.

idea	stick	dairy
shopping list	can	carton
aisle	box	dozen
loaf	bottle	container

1. Could you pick up a _____ of milk on the way home?
2. I've forgotten my _____ _____, but I think I remember what we need at the supermarket.
3. Fresh peaches are better, but if they're out of them, buy some in a _____.
4. Why don't we get a _____ of cookies for dessert?
5. There will be eight people at dinner, so we don't need more than a _____ rolls.
6. Get a small _____ of potato salad at the deli counter, too.
7. I need to buy some cheese. Can you tell me where the _____ section is?
8. Grab a _____ of butter from the refrigerator, please.
9. I have no _____ how to cook Thai food, but I eat it all the time.
10. Should we get a _____ of red or white wine?
11. Coffee and tea are in _____ seven.
12. Do you think that one _____ of bread is enough?

6C TAKE A CLOSER LOOK

MAKING SUGGESTIONS AND RECOMMENDATIONS

In the first dialogue, you heard Sveta suggest roast chicken or beef stew for dinner. Notice that she said *"What about...?"* to make the suggestion. Let's listen to a few more examples of this.

🎧 *I don't know what to make for dinner tonight.*
How about spaghetti?
What about warming up leftovers?

Where should we eat tonight?
Why don't we try the new Italian restaurant?

Karl is really gaining weight.
Why doesn't he go on a diet?

📖 As you can see, if you want to recommend something, you can use *What about...?* or *How about...?* You can follow that with either a noun or a longer expression with a verb in its *-ing* form:

What about that new restaurant tonight?
What about going to that new restaurant tonight?

You can express the same thing with *Why . . . ?* followed by a complete thought, but remember to put that thought in the negative form.

Why don't we go to that new restaurant tonight?

PRACTICE: MAKING SUGGESTIONS AND RECOMMENDATIONS
Turn the following statements into suggestions in question form using the hint in the parentheses.

1. Let's take the bus to work instead of the subway. (What about . . .)
2. They should say something to their boss. (Why . . .)
3. Let's go on a vacation in the Caribbean. (How about . . .)
4. She should buy a new car. (Why . . .)
5. Let's watch a little television before we go to bed. (How about . . .)
6. You should apply for a job here. (What about . . .)
7. You should stay home and cook tonight. (Why . . .)
8. We should go out to that Korean restaurant. (What about . . .)
9. You should stay a little longer. (Why . . .)
10. Let's spend a weekend in the country. (How about . . .)
11. You should find a private tutor to teach you Spanish. (Why . . .)
12. Let's throw a surprise party for her. (What about . . .)

MAY AND *MIGHT*
In the first dialogue, Richard explained to Sveta that he had to go to the bank to get money before going to the supermarket, so *"it might take . . . a while."* *Might* is one way of expressing a possibility, and *may* is another.

I may go to work tomorrow.
I might go to work tomorrow.

The difference between these two statements is just a matter of degree of possibility; *may* is more possible than *might*.

It may rain tomorrow. (There's a good chance that it will rain tomorrow.)
It might rain tomorrow. (There's a small chance that it will rain tomorrow.)

Now let's see how *may* and *might* are used in the past tense.

He may have worked yesterday.
He might have worked yesterday.
It may have rained last week.
It might have rained last week.

Notice that you just use *may have* or *might have* plus the past participle of the main verb. That's usually the form that ends in *–ed* (talked, worked, rained) but it can be irregular, too. We'll see much more of that in the next lesson.

PRACTICE: *MAY* AND *MIGHT*
Rewrite each of the following sentences using *may* or *might*. Use the clues provided to help you make your choice.

1. The sky is very cloudy—it _____ rain! (It's very possible.)
2. The sky is clear, but it still _____ rain. (There's a small chance.)
3. John was very sick today, so he _____ not come to work tomorrow. (There's a good chance he won't.)
4. Susan said she thinks she'll be able to meet us tonight, but she _____ be a bit late. (There's a small chance that she'll be late.)
5. No one's answering the phone. Do you think they _____ have gone out to eat? (It's not very likely.)
6. It's late. They _____ already have gone to sleep. (It's likely.)
7. It doesn't look like it, but it _____ snow tomorrow. (There's a small possibility.)
8. Greta isn't sure yet, but she _____ go to Costa Rica on vacation. (There's a small chance.)
9. I didn't sleep well at all last night; I _____ take a little nap. (It's probable.)
10. It's already 8:30; the store _____ be closed. (There's a good chance.)

6D LISTENING EXERCISE

Listen to the following suggestions and the cues at the end of each sentence. Restate using those cues.

1. *How about beef stew for dinner tonight?* (roast chicken)
2. *How about beef stew for dinner tonight?* (ham sandwiches)
3. *What about chocolate cake for dessert?* (a hot fudge sundae)
4. *What about chocolate cake for dessert?* (fruit salad)
5. *Why don't you go to the bank first?* (supermarket)
6. *Why don't you go to the bank first?* (shopping)

ANSWER KEY—PRACTICE SECTIONS

VOCABULARY

1. carton	4. box	7. dairy	10. bottle
2. shopping list	5. dozen	8. stick	11. aisle
3. can	6. container	9. idea	12. loaf

MAKING SUGGESTIONS AND RECOMMENDATIONS

1. What about taking the bus to work instead of the subway?
2. Why don't they say something to their boss?
3. How about (going on) a vacation in the Caribbean?
4. Why doesn't she buy a new car?
5. How about (watching) a little television before we go to bed?
6. What about applying for a job here?
7. Why don't you stay home and cook tonight?
8. What about going out to that Korean restaurant?
9. Why don't you stay a little longer?
10. How about (spending) a weekend in the country?
11. Why don't you find a private tutor to teach you Spanish?
12. What about throwing a surprise party for her?

MAY AND MIGHT

1. may	4. might	7. might	10. may
2. might	5. might	8. might	
3. may	6. may	9. may	

LISTENING EXERCISE

1. How about roast chicken for dinner tonight?
2. How about ham sandwiches for dinner tonight?
3. What about a hot fudge sundae for dessert?
4. What about fruit salad for dessert?
5. Why don't you go to the supermarket first?
6. Why don't you go shopping first?

Lesson 7

A JOB INTERVIEW

In Lesson 7 you'll listen to a job interview and hear about a position in a financial company. The vocabulary you'll learn will come in handy if you go on a job interview, no matter what type of position you're applying for. After the vocabulary section, you'll review how to make polite requests or ask questions in a more formal situation, and you'll take a closer look at a sentence with *if* and *would*. Finally, you'll review the present perfect tense (*has talked, have worked*) and irregular past participles (*gone, spoken, been*).

7A DIALOGUE

I'M IMPRESSED WITH YOUR RESUME

Maria Ramon is interviewing John Saunders for a position as head broker for a small financial company. Let's listen in.

Maria Ramon: *Please have a seat, Mr. Saunders. I received your résumé a few weeks ago, and I must say I'm very impressed.*

John Saunders: *Thank you.*

Maria Ramon: *We're a small financial company, trading mostly stocks and bonds. May I ask why you're interested in working for us?*

John Saunders: *Your company has an impressive reputation. And I've always wanted to work for a smaller company.*

Maria Ramon: *That's good to hear! Would you mind telling me a little bit about your present job?*

John Saunders: *I'm a head broker in a large international company. I deal with clients on a daily basis, handling all aspects of their accounts personally.*

Maria Ramon: *Why do you think you are the right candidate for this position?*

John Saunders: *I have a lot of experience in the stock market. And I enjoy working with people. As a matter of fact, in my current job I'm in charge of a team of eight brokers.*

Maria Ramon: *Well, you might just be the person we've been looking for. Do you have any questions?*

John Saunders: *Yes. If I were hired, how many accounts would I be handling?*

Maria Ramon: *You'd be working with two other head brokers. In other words, you'd be handling about a third of our clients.*

John Saunders: *And whom would I report to?*

Maria Ramon: *Directly to me.*

John Saunders: *I see. What kind of benefit package do you offer?*

Maria Ramon: *Two weeks of paid vacation in your first year of employment. I believe you're also eligible for medical and dental insurance. But this is something you should discuss with our personnel department. Do you have any other questions?*

John Saunders: *No, not at the moment.*

Maria Ramon: *Well, I'll have to discuss your application with my colleagues, and we'll get back to you early next week.*

John Saunders: *OK, thanks. It was very nice to meet you.*

Maria Ramon: *It was nice meeting you, too, and thanks for coming in today.*

Now listen to the dialogue again and repeat in the pauses.

7B WORDS IN ACTION

📖 *application*
If you're interested in this position, send in your application.

résumé
A résumé lists your education and job experience.

trade
John wants to work for a company that trades stocks and bonds.
Melissa traded her candy bar for Cindy's cookie.
Auto repair is an important trade; cars always need to be repaired.

cover letter
Your application should include a cover letter and a résumé.

impressive
Omar has a lot of experience; his résumé is impressive.
The team worked very hard on the report, and the director found it impressive.

interview
Only the most qualified candidates will be invited for an interview.

handle
Cynthia handles all of the accounts in the region.
The job was too hard for Keith to handle; he quit after three weeks.
The problem was much too difficult for her to get a handle on—she needed help understanding it.

communication skills
I have excellent written and verbal communication skills.

candidate
There are usually only two candidates for President of the United States.
There were many qualified candidates for the position.

responsibilities
My responsibilities include developing a client base.

experience
Suzanne has worked in banking for twenty-three years; she has a lot of experience.
Hector's trip to India was an amazing experience.

report to
Mrs. Richardson is my boss—I report to her.

benefits
Our benefits include medical and dental insurance.

eligible
Because Fatima is older than 65, she's eligible for a special discount.

🎧 Now listen and repeat the words and examples in bold.

PRACTICE: VOCABULARY

📖 application   interviews   experience
    résumés   handle   reports to
    trades   communication skills   benefits
    cover letter   candidate   eligible
    impressive   responsibilities

1. Chikako is always very busy at work; she has many _____.
2. Troy wants to hire a new assistant, so he's been reading a lot of _____ lately.
3. Sarah speaks clearly and writes very well. She has good _____ _____.
4. The salary is great, but there are no dental _____.
5. Kevin is unhappy because he _____ _____ a new boss who's younger than he is.
6. If you want to work here, just fill out an _____ and leave it with the receptionist.
7. Gary has a very _____ job title, so people think his position is important.
8. Joseph bought a new suit because he's going on four different _____ next week.
9. If you send your résumé to a company, always include a _____ _____.
10. Pavel works on Wall Street and _____ stocks.
11. I have a problem and I need your advice on how to _____ it.
12. Jessica interviewed a lot of people for the job, but she didn't think any of them was a strong _____ for the position.
13. After six months you're _____ for paid vacation.
14. Tina applied for the job, but they said she didn't have enough _____.

7C   TAKE A CLOSER LOOK

POLITE QUESTIONS AND REQUESTS
A job interview is obviously a situation where you would hear or use a lot of polite requests and questions. First, let's listen to three examples of polite questions.

🎧 *Do you want some coffee?*
    Would you like some coffee?
    Would you care for some coffee?

📖 You can make the simple question *Do you want . . . ?* much more polite by saying *Would you like . . . ?* or *Would you care for . . . ?*

    Would you like to go for a walk?
    Would you care for a drink?

Now let's take a closer look at polite requests. If you want to ask for something, it may sound rude to simply say *give me . . .* or *show me . . .* Of course, the easiest way to make a request polite is to add *please*. Or you could use *would you . . .* or *would you mind . . .* Let's listen to a few examples.

🎧 **Show me your résumé, please.**
Would you show me your résumé, please?
Would you mind closing the door?

📖 Here are a few more examples of polite requests. Instead of just saying *pass the sugar*, you could say:

Pass the sugar, please.
Would you pass the sugar?
Would you mind passing the sugar?
Could you pass the sugar?
Could you please pass the sugar?

PRACTICE: POLITE QUESTIONS AND REQUESTS
Fill in the blanks in the following polite requests. There may be more than one correct answer.

1. Would you _____ wait for a moment?
2. _____ you mind holding the door for a second?
3. _____ you _____ turn down the volume on the TV?
4. _____ send the letter tomorrow.
5. _____ you mind picking up the dry cleaning, _____?
6. Take this form to Mrs. Serrano's office, _____.
7. _____ you _____ tell me where the post office is?
8. _____ you mind helping me get my luggage down?

IF . . . WOULD
In the dialogue you heard John ask "*If I were hired, how many accounts would I be handling?*" This is a very common construction, technically called the unreal conditional. Let's listen to two more examples of it before we take a closer look.

🎧 **If I were hired, would I be handling all of your accounts?**
If you were hired, you'd be reporting directly to me.

📖 In the examples above, the person asking the question has not been hired yet—he's asking about a situation that's technically called a hypothetical or unreal condition, so he uses *if* and *would*. Let's look at some more examples:

(I don't speak Japanese, but . . .) If I spoke Japanese, I would go to Tokyo.
(You don't live here, but . . .) If you lived here, you would be my neighbor.
(She's not rich, but . . .) If she were rich, she would live in a much bigger house.

(We don't have the time, but . . .) If we had the time, we'd stop for coffee.
(I have to work, but . . .) If I didn't have to work, I'd go to the beach.

Did you notice that after *if* you use a verb in the past tense? *If I spoke, if you lived, if she were, if we had, if I didn't have . . .* And in the second part of the sentence, you just use *would* plus a verb in its basic form: *I would go, you would be, she would live, we'd stop, I'd go . . .*

Just remember that in conditional expressions using *be*, you should use *were* instead of *was*.

If I were you, I wouldn't say such things!
If I weren't sick today, I'd come to work.
If you were a better cook, you wouldn't burn everything!
If she were kinder, she wouldn't criticize my cooking.
If he weren't so tired, he'd come to the movies with us.

PRACTICE: *IF . . . WOULD* 1
Complete each of the following sentences by choosing the right words for each blank.

1. If he _____ (spoke/speaks) Russian he would travel to Moscow.
2. If you _____ (take/took) the train to work you wouldn't worry about traffic.
3. If they _____ (live/lived) in the country they would have a bigger house.
4. If I _____ (was/were) a better cook I would make dinner for you.
5. If he _____ (were/was) a friend he would tell you the truth.
6. If they _____ (studied/study) more they would get better grades.
7. If we _____ (eat/ate) in a restaurant every night we would have no money!
8. If she _____ (was/were) a better driver I wouldn't be afraid to ride in her car!
9. If they _____ (came/come) on time more often, we wouldn't have to wait so long!
10. If Frank _____ (was/were) a stronger employee, he would get a raise.

PRACTICE: *IF . . . WOULD* 2
Now make positive conditional sentences using the following negative clues. For example, if you see:

Sarah does not have experience. She does not have an impressive résumé.

You would form the sentence:

If Sarah had experience, she would have an impressive résumé.

1. John does not work for my company. I do not know him.
2. They do not have good benefits. I do not want to work for them.
3. You are not my boss. I do not report to you.
4. They do not have the money. They will not go to Spain for vacation.
5. We do not have the time. We will not stay longer.
6. I am not tired. I will not go to bed early.
7. I do not speak Italian. I do not understand the movie.
8. We do not leave the apartment at 8:30 every morning. We do not always get to work on time.
9. Sarah does not live close to the office. She doesn't walk to work.
10. Frida isn't going to the party. You will not see her later.

THE PRESENT PERFECT TENSE

In the dialogue you heard John Saunders say "*I've always wanted to work for a smaller company.*" Did you notice the verb tense that he used? *Have wanted* is an example of the present perfect tense. Take a look at these other examples:

Keith has never been to Tokyo before.
We've already gone to that restaurant this week—let's go somewhere else!
So far this year Wendy has traveled to San Francisco, Vancouver, and Seattle.

As you can see from the examples, the actions in each of the sentences (*being, going,* and *traveling*) happened in the past. But take another look at those examples. There are other clues about time in each of them—*never before, this week, so far this year.* What can you say about those time clues? They're unfinished. *This week* and *this year* are obviously unfinished time, and *never before* means during Keith's life, which is of course unfinished.

You'll often hear time clues similar to these when the present perfect is used. You may hear: *today, this week, this month, this year, so far, yet, already, ever, never, always* . . . all time clues that are unfinished. So, you should use the present perfect when the action is complete and in the past, but the time frame is unfinished. Let's see some more examples:

Have you ever been to Canada?
I've worked three days this week.
Have you spoken to Mr. Jacobson yet?
We've already been here!
Pete has always wanted to learn to play the guitar.
I've cleaned the house, cooked, gone jogging, and done the laundry —and it's only noon!

To form the present perfect tense, as you know, you use either *have* or *has* plus a form of the verb called the past participle. Most past participles are formed with –ed: *walked, wanted, worked, traveled.* But there are also a lot of very common verbs with irregular past participles. Let's review them now:

be – been: *Have you ever been on a horse before?*
beat – beaten: *They've never beaten us!*
become – become: *Has the water become warm enough yet?*
begin – begun: *It looks like it's begun to rain.*
bite – bitten: *Help! A snake has bitten me!*
bleed – bled: *Someone had bled on the carpet.*
blow – blown: *Wait—the birthday girl hasn't blown out the candles yet.*
break – broken: *You've broken my heart!*
bring – brought: *I'm sorry I haven't brought your CD back yet.*
broadcast – broadcast: *They've broadcast that interview twice already.*
build – built: *Someone has built a fire in the woods.*
buy – bought: *Have you bought that car you were looking at yet?*
catch – caught: *No one has caught the thief yet.*
choose – chosen: *The diners haven't chosen what they want to eat yet.*
come – come: *Kids, has your father come home from work yet?*
cost – cost: *Gas has never cost so much.*
cut – cut: *I need a bandage. I've cut my finger.*
dig – dug: *Someone has dug a hole in the yard!*
do – done: *Have the students done all of their homework yet?*
draw – drawn: *I've never drawn before, but I'd like to take an art course.*
drink – drunk: *You haven't drunk all of your juice yet.*
drive – driven: *I've driven twice around the block looking for your house.*
eat – eaten: *We've eaten at this restaurant before; it's very good.*
fall – fallen: *Why are you afraid of horses? Have you fallen from one before?*
feed – fed: *Has anyone fed the dog yet?*
feel – felt: *I've never felt so guilty about something in my life!*
fight – fought: *They've fought hard to get the project done.*
find – found: *Has anyone found a gold bracelet in the bathroom?*
fly – flown: *I've never flown this airline before; it's very nice!*
forget – forgotten: *Don't worry—I haven't forgotten to call him back.*
forgive – forgiven: *Have you forgiven me yet?*
freeze – frozen: *The lake hasn't frozen yet, but it's already very cold.*
get – gotten: *Have they gotten up yet, or are they still sleeping?*
give – given: *Who's given you a Christmas gift already? It's only December 10th!*
go – gone: *Have you gone to Mexico on business yet?*
grow – grown: *Look! The plants have grown so much already!*
hang – hung: *We've already hung the decorations, so you can help us set up the chairs.*
have – had: *I've had enough!*
hear – heard: *Have you heard the news yet?*
hold – held: *Theresa wants to hold the baby. She hasn't held him yet.*

keep – kept: I've kept my promise.
know – known: I've never known anyone from Portugal.
lay – laid: Have they laid the carpet in the living room yet?
leave – left: Why has everyone left?
let – let: Our boss has never let us leave early.
lie – lain: It's 2:00; we've lain here on the beach for three hours already.
lose – lost: Has anyone lost a wallet? I found one on the stairs.
make – made: Have you made up your mind yet?
meet – met: We still haven't met—I'm Paul Cooper.
mistake – mistaken: You've mistaken me for someone else.
pay – paid: Have you paid the plumber yet?
put – put: I've already put in a good word for you.
quit – quit: We haven't quit the game yet; there's still hope.
read (pronounced "reed") – read (pronounced "red"): Have you read this book already? It's good.
ride – ridden: Mr. Mendez has ridden this train every day for thirty years.
ring – rung: Has the bell rung yet?
rise – risen: The sun hasn't even risen yet! Let's go back to bed.
run – run: We've run out of gas.
say – said: Has she said "yes" yet?
see – seen: They've never seen that show on television here.
sell – sold: Have you sold your boat yet? I want to buy it!
send – sent: I've already sent the letter.
shoot – shot: The actor yelled, "Someone has shot me!"
shut – shut: You haven't shut the door yet. You need to push harder.
sing – sung: I've never sung before so many people in my life. I'm scared.
sink – sunk: The ship hasn't sunk yet, but it will sink soon.
sit – sat: We've sat around and talked for too long. Let's go outside.
sleep – slept: No one has slept in this bed yet—it's still made.
speak – spoken: Mrs. Ewing has spoken very highly of you.
spend – spent: I've spent all of my money.
stand – stood: They've stood there for hours.
steal – stolen: Your car is still there—no one has stolen it.
swim – swum: Have you ever swum in the Pacific Ocean?
take – taken: I haven't taken my lunch break yet.
teach – taught: Has your father taught you to drive yet?
tear – torn: I can't wear that shirt—someone has torn a hole in it.
tell – told: Have I told you about my friend Jack before?
think – thought: You haven't thought this through yet, have you?
throw – thrown: Look! Someone has thrown all of these books away.
understand – understood: She still hasn't understood what I mean.
wear – worn: Have you worn your new suit yet?
win – won: It's halfway through the season, and we haven't won a single game.
write – written: Winston hasn't written his report yet.

PRACTICE: THE PRESENT PERFECT TENSE

Fill in each of the following blanks using the correct form of the verb in parentheses.

1. Has your mother _____ to work yet kids? (go)
2. They've _____ a lot this summer. (swim)
3. What have you _____ so far during your trip to New York? (do)
4. We've _____ the Empire State Building, the Statue of Liberty, and Broadway. (see)
5. How many times have they _____ about the proposal? (talk)
6. Have you _____ for dinner yet? (pay)
7. Someone has _____ a hole in the table cloth. (tear)
8. Has the film _____ yet? (begin)
9. You kids have already _____ too much television! (watch)
10. What have you _____ from the wine list? (choose)
11. It's really _____ cold these past few days. (get)
12. Wow! I've never _____ so alive! (feel)
13. Has anyone _____ a watch? (lose)
14. Have you _____ your dinner yet? (finish)
15. I've never _____ someone so interesting. (know)
16. Has she ever _____ a horse before? (ride)
17. The secretary has already _____ out the mail. (send)
18. The movie hasn't _____ yet. (start)
19. I haven't _____ anyone their gifts yet. (give)
20. They've already _____ their names on the list. (write)

7D LISTENING EXERCISE

🎧 Listen to the recorded sentences, and restate them as polite questions or requests using the cues provided.

1. *Do you want to come in for an interview?* (like)
2. *Send in your résumé, please.* (mind)
3. *Call me next week.* (would)
4. *Please discuss this with personnel.* (mind)

ANSWER KEY—PRACTICE SECTIONS

VOCABULARY

1. responsibilities	4. benefits	8. interviews	12. candidate
2. résumés	5. reports to	9. cover letter	13. eligible
3. communication	6. application	10. trades	14. experience
	7. impressive skills	11. handle	

POLITE QUESTIONS AND REQUESTS

1. please	3. Would, Could . . .	5. Would . . . please	7. Would, Could . . .
2. Would	4. Please	6. please	8. Would

IF . . . WOULD 1

1. spoke	4. were	7. ate	9. came
2. took	5. were	8. were	10. were
3. lived	6. studied		

IF . . . WOULD 2

1. If John worked for my company I would know him.
2. If they had good benefits I would want to work for them.
3. If you were my boss I would report to you.
4. If they had the money they would go to Spain for vacation.
5. If we had the time we would stay longer.
6. If I were tired I would go to bed early.
7. If I spoke Italian I would understand the movie.
8. If we left the apartment at 8:30 every morning we would always get to work on time.
9. If Sarah lived close to the office she would walk to work.
10. If Frida were going to the party you would see her later.

THE PRESENT PERFECT TENSE

1. gone	6. paid	11. gotten	16. ridden
2. swum	7. torn	12. felt	17. sent
3. done	8. begun	13. lost	18. started
4. seen	9. watched	14. finished	19. given
5. talked	10. chosen	15. known	20. written

LISTENING EXERCISE

1. Would you like to come in for an interview?
2. Would you mind sending in your résumé?
3. Would you call me next week?
4. Would you mind discussing this with personnel?

Lesson 8

THE FIRST DAY IN THE OFFICE

As you can see from its title, Lesson 8 is about working. First you'll hear a dialogue about someone's first day in a new office, so you'll learn vocabulary that deals with offices, working, and companies in general. Then you'll take a closer look at the uses of the very common verb *must*. After that you'll review possessives, or words like *my* and *mine*, *your* and *yours*, and so on. Finally, you'll review the simple past tense (*went* instead of *has gone*), especially those irregular verbs.

8A DIALOGUE

YOU MUST BE OUR NEW COLLEAGUE!

Today is Bob Fuller's first day at his new office. He's beginning a job in the international sales division, and he's meeting some of his new colleagues. Let's listen in as one of them introduces him to some of the people he'll work with.

🎧
Susan Richter:	*Hi, I'm Susan Richter. And you must be Bob.*
Bob Fuller:	*Yes, Bob Fuller. Nice to meet you.*
Susan Richter:	*Let me introduce you to some people. Annette, I'd like you to meet our new colleague.*
Annette Silva:	*Oh, hello, I'm Annette Silva. Good to meet you.*
Bob Fuller:	*Hi, I'm Bob Fuller.*
Annette Silva:	*Where will you be working?*
Bob Fuller:	*In the international sales division.*
Annette Silva:	*Oh, right next door. We'll be seeing a lot of each other then. Let's have lunch sometime.*
Bob Fuller:	*Yes, I'd love to.*
Susan Richter:	*Let me introduce you to Phil now. He's the manager of our division.*
Phil Mendez:	*Hey, you must be Bob. We've been expecting you. I'm Phil Mendez.*
Bob Fuller:	*Nice to meet you.*
Phil Mendez:	*Welcome aboard.*

Now listen to the dialogue again and repeat in the pauses.

📖 A little while later, after Bob settles in a bit, he speaks to the manager of his division, Phil Mendez.

🎧
Phil Mendez:	*So, how was your commute this morning?*
Bob Fuller:	*Not bad at all. It took me only twenty minutes to get here. By the way, I was wondering about my hours. I arrived here at nine today. Would it be better if I got here earlier on some days?*
Phil Mendez:	*Yes. Would you mind getting here around 8:30?*
Bob Fuller:	*Not at all. And when do you usually leave, 5:00?*
Phil Mendez:	*Well, we usually leave when the work's done. Sometimes that's 6:00 or even later. Let's play it by ear.*
Bob Fuller:	*No problem. And one more thing. Could you tell me how the telephone works?*
Phil Mendez:	*Sure. Dial 9 for an outside line, and then the number you are calling. If you want to contact anyone in the office, just dial their extension.*
Bob Fuller:	*OK. Thanks.*

Listen to the dialogue a second time, and repeat in the pauses provided.

8B   WORDS IN ACTION

 colleague
She's always at work. She spends more time with her colleagues than her family!

manager
I must find out what my manager wants me to do today.

division
There are twenty-five people in my division. We all work on sales.

sales
Jonah works for the sales division; he meets with his accounts to sell the company's merchandise.

advertising
The advertising department makes ads for television and magazines.

I.T. (Information Technology)
If your computer isn't working, call I.T.

publicity
The author was interviewed on television—that's good publicity.

marketing
The marketing department works closely with sales, publicity, and advertising.

accounting (finance)
Billing and payments are handled by the accounting (finance) department.

human resources
Human resources is in charge of hiring employees.

fax
No one mails letters today—everyone just sends faxes.

dial
For long-distance calls, dial '1' first.

extension
I don't know Kevin's extension, so I called the general number of his company.

line
The line is busy; I'll call back later.

to play it by ear
There are no set working hours; we'll play it by ear.

"Let's have lunch."
We haven't talked in ages. Let's have lunch soon.

reception
When you first enter an office, you arrive in the reception area.

commute
My commute isn't bad at all; it only takes me twenty minutes to get to work.

e-mail
Send the report by e-mail; it's much faster than mail.
She e-mailed me all of the travel information.

aboard
Welcome to our company, welcome aboard!

Now turn on the recordings and listen to the vocabulary in bold. Repeat each word or expression, and the example sentence, in the pauses provided.

PRACTICE: VOCABULARY

colleagues	I.T. (Information	extension
manager	Technology)	play it by ear
divisions	publicity	reception
sales	accounting	commute
marketing	human resources	e-mail
advertising	fax	on board
	dial	

1. There's a _____ coming through for you, Bob, but the machine is out of paper.
2. The company scandal was in all of the newspapers and created a lot of bad _____.
3. When you come into the building go to the _____ area and say that you have an appointment with Mr. Krauss.
4. Linda's a good _____. Everyone who reports to her likes her, and they get their jobs done well.
5. I see a lot of my _____ in this restaurant for lunch, since it's so close to where we work.
6. Tina wants to work for that company, so she sent her résumé to the _____ _____ department.
7. The _____ department develops commercials for television and ads for magazines.
8. We work for the same company, but since we're in different _____ we never see each other at work.
9. The international _____ division handles all of the accounts outside the U.S.
10. Henry's great with computers, so he's perfect for the _____ _____ department.
11. Send the bill to the _____ department so that they can pay it.
12. What's your _____? I only have the general number.

13. _____ '9' to get an outside line.
14. Send me an _____; I need the information right away.
15. I'm happy to be _____ _____ with a new company!
16. My _____ is horrible! It takes me two hours to get to work every day.
17. I'm not sure of the details yet—let's just _____ _____ _____ _____.
18. The new _____ plan has been very successful—everyone knows about the product.

8C TAKE A CLOSER LOOK

USES OF *MUST*
In the dialogue you heard Susan Richter say, *"You must be Bob."* Must is a word you hear a lot in English. Let's talk about some of the different ways you can use it. First, turn on your CD and listen to a few examples.

🎧 *You haven't called him yet?*
You must call him immediately.
You worked all day?
You must be tired.
Tom hasn't come in yet?
He must be sick.
We must be early.
No one else is here yet.
Richard lives out of town?
His commute must be terrible.

📖 Of course, *must* can be used to mean "have to."

I have to finish this report and give it to my manager by tomorrow!
I must finish this report and give it to my manager by tomorrow!

But in the examples above, you heard that *must* can also be used to mean things like "probably" or "I'm sure that . . ." or "I assume that . . ."

The ground is all wet! It must have rained during the night.
(It probably rained.)
It's 3:00 in the morning. They must all be asleep!
(I'm sure they're all asleep!)
You haven't eaten since the morning? You must be hungry!
(I assume you're hungry.)

PRACTICE: USES OF *MUST*
Rewrite each of the following sentences using *must*.

1. I assume that you're John.
2. It's probably very cold outside.

3.   I'm sure that she's our new manager.
4.   I assume that you work in the sales division.
5.   It's probably snowing in the mountains.
6.   I'm sure that they're getting home right now.
7.   I assume that you're my new neighbor.
8.   It's certain that the kids are upset about the rain on their vacation.

POSSESSIVES

Susan introduced Bob as *"our new colleague."* Let's take a moment to review all of the possessives. As you know, *my, your, his, her, its, our,* and *their* are used right before nouns to show who they belong to.

My commute is great; I live around the corner!
Who's the head of your department?
His name is John Franken.
Her assistant sent me the files.
The company is not proud of its publicity!
Their reputation has been awful.

There's another set of possessives that never come right before nouns. *Mine, yours, his, hers, ours* and *theirs* are pronouns—you use them to replace nouns. Take a look at these examples:

Jerry's commute is great. How's yours?
Mine is not so good. Traffic is always bad.
This division is more interesting than his.
But hers makes the most money.
Mary's company is better known than ours.
The file here is theirs.

PRACTICE: POSSESSIVES

Choose the right possessive for each of the following sentences.

1.   Your office is bigger than _____ (my/mine).
2.   Joan gave _____ (her/hers) assistant too much work to do.
3.   The people in the sales division don't like _____ (their/theirs) manager.
4.   _____ (Ours/Our) is a much better manager.
5.   Who's _____ (your/yours) boss?
6.   This is _____ (my/mine) notebook. Where's _____ (your/yours)?
7.   _____ (Their/Theirs) department is much busier than _____ (our/ours).
8.   This is _____ (their/theirs) first time working in an office.
9.   _____ (My/Mine) last job didn't last very long.
10. If he doesn't have a laptop, lend him _____ (your/yours).

VERBS IN THE PAST TENSE

In the last chapter you took a look at the present perfect tense. Now let's focus on the simple past. You heard a few examples of verbs in the simple past tense in the dialogue:

So, how was your commute this morning?
It only took me twenty minutes to get here.
I arrived here at nine today.

The simple past tense is used when both the action and the time are finished. As you know, it's easy to form most verbs in the past tense. They're like *arrived*; you just add *–d* or *–ed* to the verb:

We talked for hours last night.
The marketing department developed a new plan last month.
We e-mailed them our résumés last week.

Notice that some consonants double up when you add *–ed*:

He submitted the report on time.
We wrapped his present in recycled paper.
I dropped the jar on the way to the sink and it shattered.

To form a negative sentence or questions in the simple past tense, use *did* or *didn't* and the verb in its basic form.

We didn't talk at all last night.
Did the marketing department develop a new plan?
We didn't e-mail them our résumés.
Didn't he submit the report on time?

You may also hear people asking questions that used changed intonation to express shock or disbelief. These questions retain the simple past tense form of the verb and do not use *did* or *didn't*:

You wrapped his present in recycled paper? How resourceful!
You dropped the jar? It was an antique!

There are many verbs—very common verbs—that have irregular past tenses, like *was* and *took*. These just have to be memorized. You probably know most of them, but let's review the more common ones. Let's start with *be*, which of course has the forms *was* and *were*.

I was at the office while all of you were home.
We were awake all night.

You don't need to use *did* for questions or the negative of *be*:

I wasn't at the office.
We weren't at work on time this morning.
Was he at school when you were there?
Weren't they best friends?

Now let's look at some of the others. The first few examples also include the negative.

beat – beat: They beat our team. They didn't beat our team.
become – became: He became angry. He didn't become angry.
begin – began: It began to rain yesterday. It didn't begin to rain yesterday.
bite – bit: Your dog bit me! Your dog didn't bite me.
bleed – bled: I have a cut, and I bled on my new shirt. I didn't bleed ...
blow – blew: The wind blew all night long. The wind didn't blow ...
break – broke: I think I broke my new computer somehow. I didn't break ...
bring – brought: They brought the sales up.
broadcast – broadcast: They broadcast the news on the radio.
build – built: She built the house herself.
buy – bought: We bought a new car last month.
catch – caught: The police caught the criminals.
choose – chose: I chose this company for its reputation.
come – came: We came home late last night.
cost – cost: That coat cost too much.
cut – cut: We cut our costs in half.
dig – dug: He really dug himself into a hole!
do – did: You did the right thing.
draw – drew: I drew this picture. Do you like it?
drink – drank: They drank all of the milk.
drive – drove: We drove to California last month.
eat – ate: I ate early last night and watched television.
fall – fell: The temperature fell during the night.
feed – fed: I fed the dog before work.
feel – felt: It felt a bit strange in the meeting.
fight – fought: They fought during the entire trip.
find – found: I found the book interesting.
fly – flew: We flew to London last night.
forget – forgot: You forgot my birthday!
forgive – forgave: He finally forgave us after a few hours.
freeze – froze: It was so cold that the lake froze.
get – got: It got much warmer last week.
give – gave: They gave you a great gift.
go – went: She went to Mexico for the training.
grow – grew: I grew up near New York.
hang – hung: He hung his coat behind the door.

have – had: We had a great time.
hear – heard: They heard the bad news.
hold – held: They held their new baby all the time.
keep – kept: You kept the reports in the filing cabinet.
know – knew: I knew her when she worked here.
lay – laid: They laid the towels on the beach.
leave – left: She left early yesterday.
let – let: We let him stay here too long.
lie – lay: We lay on the beach all day long.
lose – lost: I lost my cell phone.
make – made: You made the right decision.
meet – met: I think you met my boyfriend.
mistake – mistook: I mistook her for a client, but she's my new manager.
pay – paid: We paid much too much for that meal!
put – put: I put it on my credit card.
quit – quit: He quit his job yesterday.
read (pronounced "reed") *– read* (pronounced "red"): I read all about it in the newspaper.
ride – rode: I rode the subway to work.
ring – rang: The telephone rang at 4:00 in the morning.
rise – rose: The sun rose at 6:42 this morning.
run – ran: We ran out of ideas at the meeting.
say – said: My mother said I should have studied medicine.
see – saw: They saw the plan before we did.
sell – sold: The Richardson's sold their house and moved away.
send – sent: He sent me an e-mail, but I haven't opened it.
shoot – shot: The policeman shot in the air.
shut – shut: I shut the door so we could speak privately.
sing – sang: She sang at my retirement party.
sink – sank: The boat sank, but the passengers were rescued.
sit – sat: She sat next to me at the meeting.
sleep – slept: I slept for eight hours last night.
speak – spoke: He spoke too long at the ceremony.
spend – spent: I spent all of my savings on this present!
stand – stood: You stood there in the rain?
steal – stole: Someone stole my purse from my office.
swim – swam: I went to the gym and swam at lunch.
take – took: She took a long time to get to work.
teach – taught: Who taught you that?
tear – tore: I tore up the report.
tell – told: My boss told me to be in early today.
think – thought: We thought you worked in another division.
throw – threw: They threw away all of the old files.
understand – understood: She understood what I said.
wear – wore: You wore that to an interview?

win – won: Who won the contest?
write – wrote: I wrote a long letter.

PRACTICE: VERBS IN THE PAST TENSE

Rewrite the following sentences in the past tense. For example, if you see "*I go to the movies,*" you'd rewrite the sentence as "*I went to the movies.*"

1.   She thinks about her friend.
2.   The advertising department spends a lot of money.
3.   John e-mails his friend about the trip.
4.   They sleep for nine hours.
5.   Jason takes the bus to go to his interview.
6.   Lisa starts working in the sales division on Monday.
7.   We don't take the bus to work every day.
8.   Annette sees Harry a lot.
9.   Julia does her shopping in the afternoon.
10. Hector chooses his wine carefully.

8D LISTENING EXERCISE

🎧 Listen to the recorded sentences and rephrase them using *must*.

1.   *You're probably our new colleague, Richard.*
2.   *I'm sure the phone book is on my desk.*
3.   *I probably left my keys at home.*
4.   *He's probably sick.*
5.   *I assume you're hungry.*

ANSWER KEY—PRACTICE SECTIONS

VOCABULARY

1. fax	7. advertising	11. accounting	15. on board
2. publicity	8. divisions	12. extension	16. commute
3. reception	9. sales	13. Dial	17. play it by ear
4. manager	10. I.T./Information Technology	14. e-mail	18. marketing
5. colleagues			
6. human resources			

USES OF MUST

1. You must be John.
2. It must be very cold outside.
3. She must be our new manager.
4. You must work in the sales division.
5. It must be snowing in the mountains.
6. They must be getting home right now.
7. You must be my new neighbor.
8. The kids must be upset about the rain on their vacation.

POSSESSIVES

1. mine	4. Ours	7. Their, ours	9. My
2. her	5. your	8. their	10. yours
3. their	6. my, yours		

VERBS IN THE PAST TENSE

1. She thought about her friend.
2. The advertising department spent a lot of money.
3. John e-mailed his friend about the trip.
4. They slept for nine hours.
5. Jason took the bus to go to his interview.
6. Lisa started working in the sales division on Monday.
7. We didn't take the bus to work every day.
8. Annette saw Harry a lot.
9. Julia did her shopping in the afternoon.
10. Hector chose his wine carefully.

LISTENING EXERCISE

1. You must be our new colleague, Richard.
2. The phone book must be on my desk.
3. I must have left my keys at home.
4. He must be sick.
5. You must be hungry.

Lesson 9

A BUSINESS MEETING

As you can guess from the name of the lesson, Lesson 9 will take you to a business meeting. You'll listen in as two businessmen discuss the costs of a proposal, so you'll hear plenty of important vocabulary that deals with money and business in general. Then you'll review the uses of *must, need to, have to, had better*, and *should*. After that, you'll also take a closer look at the present perfect continuous, which is the form of the verb you see in sentences such as *I have been studying for hours* or *We have been living here for ten years*.

9A DIALOGUE

LET'S GO OVER THAT PROPOSAL

Let's listen as Bill Tapscott and Gary Mann discuss a proposal for new business strategies. Listen closely for a lot of the vocabulary you've already learned.

Bill Tapscott:	*Hello, Gary. How are you?*
Gary Mann:	*Fine! And yourself?*
Bill Tapscott:	*Can't complain. Did you have time to look at my proposal?*
Gary Mann:	*No, not really. Can we go over it now?*
Bill Tapscott:	*Sure. I've been trying to come up with some new production and advertising strategies. First of all, if we want to stay competitive, we need to modernize our factory. New equipment is long overdue.*
Gary Mann:	*How much will that cost?*
Bill Tapscott:	*We have several options ranging from one hundred thousand dollars all the way up to half a million.*
Gary Mann:	*OK. We'll have to discuss these costs with finance.*
Bill Tapscott:	*We should also consider human resources. I've been talking to personnel as well as our staff at the factories.*
Gary Mann:	*And what's the picture?*
Bill Tapscott:	*We'll probably have to hire one or two engineers to help us modernize the factory.*
Gary Mann:	*What about advertising?*
Bill Tapscott:	*Marketing has some interesting ideas for television commercials.*
Gary Mann:	*TV—isn't that a bit too expensive for us? What's wrong with advertising in the papers, as usual?*
Bill Tapscott:	*Quite frankly, it's just not enough anymore. We need to be more aggressive in order to keep ahead of our competitors.*
Gary Mann:	*Will we be able to afford all this?*
Bill Tapscott:	*I'll look into it, but I think higher costs will be justified. These investments will result in higher profits for our company.*
Gary Mann:	*We'll have to look at these figures more closely. Have finance draw up a budget for these investments.*
Bill Tapscott:	*Will do.*

Now listen to the dialogue again. This time, repeat after the native speakers in the pauses provided.

9B WORDS IN ACTION

📖 *proposal*
A proposal presents new ideas and strategies.

really
–Did you like the movie? –Not really; I thought it was boring.
I'm really thirsty! Let's get a drink.
Did she really say that? That's unbelievable!

equipment
Factory equipment is expensive but it lasts a long time.

strategy
The team's strategy was successful; they won the game.

modernize
Our equipment is old; we need to modernize.

long overdue
A new car is long overdue. We should have bought one long ago.

options
We have several options—we can advertise on TV, on the radio, or in the papers.

range
Our advertising options range from TV to radio to newspapers.

competitive
In order to stay competitive with other companies, we must modernize our production.

profits
The company had much higher profits last year; it made less money this year.

staff
There are ten people on staff at the hotel.
We're going to staff the department with employees who already have experience in the field.

investments
Wise investments will make us more competitive.
A new house is a big investment.
The stock market is not doing well; I'm worried about our investments.

aggressive
We need new ideas and an aggressive strategy to be successful.
Don't pet that dog! It's very aggressive.

budget
We have enough money for television advertisement in our budget.
You should budget some money for unexpected costs, just in case.

justified
Because the landlord renovated the apartment, he felt that a higher rent was justified.

🎧 Now turn on the recordings and listen to the vocabulary in bold. Repeat each word or expression, and the example sentence, in the pauses provided.

PRACTICE: VOCABULARY

proposal	long overdue	staff
really	options	investment
equipment	range	aggressive
strategy	competitive	budget
modernized	profits	justified

1. Ice hockey is a very _____ sport; it has to be since everything is so fast!
2. We hadn't seen each other in months! Our dinner was _____ _____.
3. I'm _____ sorry that you can't make it to the party.
4. I don't think that a higher price is _____. It's the same product!
5. Boys can be very _____ with one another. They always want to be the best.
6. The marketing department submitted a _____ that included increased advertising and publicity.
7. The company's _____ to attract younger customers includes a plan to advertise its product with rock stars and sports heroes.
8. Instead of renting, I wanted to buy a house as an _____.
9. -Does he work here? -Yes, he's on _____.
10. The _____ in the factory is very old and needs to be replaced.
11. The company is not doing very well; _____ are very low.
12. The highway system is extremely old and needs to be _____.
13. We need to make a decision now. What are our _____?
14. They publish a whole _____ of books from fiction to mysteries to popular science.
15. We spent too much money! We're far over our _____.

9C TAKE A CLOSER LOOK

MUST, NEED TO, HAVE TO, HAD BETTER, SHOULD
We've already seen many examples of how *must* is used to show not just a necessity, but also to mean the same thing as "I'm sure that..." or "I assume that..." Now let's take a look at some other expressions of necessity, obligation, and advice. First, listen to the examples on the CD.

🎧 *We need to modernize.*
We shouldn't forget to discuss this later.

We must stay competitive at all costs.
We have to stay competitive at all costs.
We had better hire new staff if we want to stay competitive.
We had better not decide without discussing this with finance.

📖 Let's start by reviewing *need*. Use *need* to show that something is necessary for some reason. You can use it to show that something is necessary because of rules or regulations, because of social expectations, or even because of neutral fact.

You need to show your boarding pass before you get on the plane.
I need to finish the report by 1:00 tomorrow.
We need to get there on time!
People need to eat and drink to stay alive.

Should is not as strong as *need*. It shows a recommendation or an expectation rather than a necessity.

You should always bring flowers or wine if you're invited to someone's house.
He should wear his blue suit when he makes the presentation.
You should speak softly when you're in a library.

Have to is used the same way as *must*.

I must find a new job soon. I have to find a new job soon.
She must start working on the proposal. She has to start working on the proposal.

In the negative, however, these expressions have different meanings. *Must not* means that it's necessary that you not do something:

Children, you must not play with scissors!
You mustn't light a cigarette now! We're at a gas station!

Don't have to, on the other hand, means that something isn't necessary. It's similar to *don't need to*.

You don't have to pay me now; you can give me the money later.
I don't have to be at work until 10:00 this morning.

Finally, let's take a look at *had better*. *Had better* is used to express that it's a very, very good idea to do something (or not to do something) to avoid a bad or unpleasant outcome. It's a way of giving strong advice.

You had better explain why the project is so far over budget.
We had better think of a new strategy—the one we have now is not working.
He'd better not come in late again today, or he'll be fired.
We'd better go home now; your mother will worry if we're too late.

PRACTICE: *MUST, NEED TO, HAVE TO, HAD BETTER, SHOULD*
Complete each of the following sentences.

1. People _____ (have to/should) drink water in order to live.
2. You _____ (have to/had better) turn the key to get the car to start.
3. You kids _____ (had better/should) clean this house before your mother gets home, or she'll be very angry!
4. He _____ (must not/doesn't have to) show ID to get into the building.
5. You really _____ (don't have to/shouldn't) eat that last piece of cake; don't forget you're on a diet.
6. I don't want to work, but I _____ (have to/should) if I want to pay rent!
7. I _____ (must not/don't have to) finish the project tonight—I can work on it tomorrow.
8. I haven't spoken to my sister in months. I _____ (must/had better) give her a call this weekend.
9. Jason has an interview on Monday, but his clothes are no good! He _____ (needs to/must) go to a clothing store.
10. Yolanda is lonely living on her own. She _____ (must/should) get a dog.

PRESENT PERFECT CONTINUOUS
In the dialogue you heard Bill Tapscott say *"I've been trying to come up with some new production and advertising strategies."* The tense that he uses is called the present perfect continuous. Use it when you want to talk about an action that began in the past and is still happening, without interruption. For example, if you started eating at 7:00, and now it's 7:30, you could say *I have been eating for thirty minutes* or *I've been eating since 7:00*. You'll often hear a time phrase with *since* or *for* with this tense.

It's easy to form the present perfect continuous—just use *have* or *has* + *been* + the *–ing* form of your verb. Let's take a look at some other examples.

She has been studying Swahili for three years.
Have you been waiting for a long time?
They haven't been speaking to each other.
We've been talking on the phone for forty minutes now!

PRACTICE: PRESENT PERFECT CONTINUOUS
Use the clues provided to change each of the following sentences from the present continuous tense to the present perfect continuous tense.

1. I am eating. (for twenty minutes.)
2. We are waiting for a table. (since 8:00.)
3. The family lives on Pleasant Grove Road. (since 1992.)

4. Ted watches the news. (for twenty-five minutes.)
5. Monica is going to college. (for the past two years.)
6. Are you living alone? (for the past four months?)
7. Who is talking on the phone? (for so long?)
8. I am working at the computer. (since I got home.)
9. The neighbor's dog barks. (for hours.)
10. The child is coughing and sneezing. (since yesterday morning.)
11. We're walking on the beach. (for the whole morning.)
12. The couple next door argues. (all night.)
13. The sun is shining. (all day.)
14. The brothers don't speak to each other. (since they got into a fight last week.)
15. Is he working on the same project? (since the last time I spoke to him.)

9D LISTENING EXERCISE

Listen to the recorded sentences and rephrase them using the cues provided.

1. *You're on time every day.* (should)
2. *He comes up with a good idea.* (had better)
3. *I'm studying English.* (need)
4. *He works much harder.* (should)
5. *Our advertising is more aggressive.* (had better)

ANSWER KEY—PRACTICE SECTIONS

VOCABULARY

1. aggressive	5. competitive	9. staff	13. options
2. long overdue	6. proposal	10. equipment	14. range
3. really	7. strategy	11. profits	15. budget
4. justified	8. investment	12. modernized	

MUST, NEED TO, HAVE TO, HAD BETTER, SHOULD

1. have to	4. doesn't have to	7. don't have to	9. needs to
2. have to	5. shouldn't	8. had better	10. should
3. had better	6. have to		

PRESENT PERFECT CONTINUOUS

1. I have been eating for twenty minutes.
2. We have been waiting for a table since 8:00.
3. The family has been living on Pleasant Grove Road since 1992.
4. Ted has been watching the news for twenty-five minutes.
5. Monica has been going to college for the past two years.
6. Have you been living alone for the past four months?
7. Who has been talking on the phone for so long?
8. I have been working at the computer since I got home.
9. The neighbor's dog has been barking for hours.
10. The child has been coughing and sneezing since yesterday morning.
11. We've been walking on the beach for the whole morning.
12. The couple next door has been arguing all night.
13. The sun has been shining all day.
14. The brothers haven't been speaking to each other since they got into a fight last week.
15. Has he been working on the same project since the last time I spoke to him?

LISTENING EXERCISE

1. You should be on time every day.
2. He had better come up with a good idea.
3. I need to study English.
4. He should work much harder.
5. Our advertising had better be more aggressive.

Lesson 10

ON THE PHONE

In Lesson 10 you'll listen in as people talk on the phone. Telephone conversations are often difficult for people who are learning a new language, so you'll hear two different dialogues—one informal, between close friends, and another one more formal, in a business setting. You'll review vocabulary related to both situations, and then you'll take a closer look at using *can* and *may*, as well as *each other* and *one another*. You'll also go over the past perfect tense, as in *I had been out of college for a whole year before I found a job*.

10A DIALOGUE

DIALOGUE 1: MAY I ASK WHO'S CALLING?

Let's listen in as Martin calls his friend Ewa to ask if she'd like to go out to dinner with him.

Anna:	*Hello?*
Martin:	*Hi, is Ewa there?*
Anna:	*May I ask who's calling?*
Martin:	*This is Martin.*
Anna:	*Hold on, I'll get her.*
Martin:	*Thanks.*
Ewa:	*Hello?*
Martin:	*Hi, Ewa, this is Martin. How are you?*
Ewa:	*Hi, how are you?*
Martin:	*Fine. I was wondering if you'd like to go out to dinner tonight?*
Ewa:	*That would be nice. Where should we go?*
Martin:	*I thought we could try that new Italian place on the corner.*
Ewa:	*Good idea. What time should we meet?*
Martin:	*Why don't I come pick you up at around seven?*
Ewa:	*I'll be ready!*

Now listen again and repeat in the pauses.

DIALOGUE 2: I'M SORRY, HE'S IN A MEETING AT THE MOMENT

This time let's listen in to a more formal dialogue. Mr. Shapiro and Mr. Tirelli are trying to reach each other by telephone, and as usual, their schedules are making it difficult. Listen as they leave messages for each other.

Mr. Tirelli's Assistant:	*Sundance Enterprises, good morning.*
Mr. Shapiro:	*Good morning. May I speak to Andrew Tirelli, please?*
Mr. Tirelli's Assistant:	*I'm sorry, Mr. Tirelli is in a meeting at the moment. Can he call you back?*
Mr. Shapiro:	*Sure thing.*
Mr. Tirelli's Assistant:	*Can I have your name and number, please?*
Mr. Shapiro:	*Yes, this is Peter Shapiro from De Mario. I'm at 873-7059.*
Mr. Tirelli's Assistant:	*I'll have him call you right back.*
Mr. Shapiro:	*Thanks.*
	(A LITTLE LATER)
Mr. Tirelli:	*Mr. Shapiro, please.*

Mr. Shapiro's
    Assistant: *I'm sorry, Mr. Shapiro just stepped away from his desk.*
                 May I take a message?
    Mr. Tirelli: *Would you ask him to call Mr. Tirelli from Sundance?*
Mr. Shapiro's
    Assistant: *May I ask what this is in reference to?*
    Mr. Tirelli: *I'm just returning his call.*
Mr. Shapiro's
    Assistant: *OK, I'll give him the message.*
    Mr. Tirelli: *Thanks, good-bye.*

Listen to the dialogue a second time, and repeat in the pauses provided.

10B WORDS IN ACTION

directory assistance
If you don't know a phone number, dial 411 for directory assistance.

message
Can I leave a message for Tom?

voice mail
I left a message for the vice president on her voice mail.

call back
I'll call Mr. Brown back tomorrow.

conference call
The account reps have a conference call scheduled for tomorrow at 9:30.

return a call
I haven't spoken to him yet; he won't return my calls.

call in
I'll be away from the office, but I'll call in for my messages.
Robert has a call in to his landlords; he's waiting for them to call him back.

reference
I'm calling in reference to your order from last week.

call waiting
Oops—that's my call waiting. Wait a moment while I take this other call.

hold on
Don't hang up. Hold on, I'll get him.

speaker phone
Don't put me on speaker phone! I don't want everyone to hear what I have to say.

cell (mobile)
I'll be walking home, so call me on my cell (mobile) phone.

calling card
Can I buy a calling card to call India from here?

pager (beeper)
If you want me to call you back, call my pager (beeper) and leave your number.

text message
You can leave me voice mail, or send me a text message.

Now turn on the recordings and listen to the vocabulary in bold. Repeat each word or expression, and the example sentence, in the pauses provided.

PRACTICE: VOCABULARY

directory assistance	call in	cell
message	reference	calling card
voice mail	call waiting	beeper
conference call	hold on	text messages
returned	speaker phone	

1. Just a second, I'm getting another call. _____ _____ can really be a nuisance!
2. The sink's broken, but I have a _____ _____ to the plumber.
3. May I leave a _____ for her?
4. Ramon bought an international _____ _____ at the deli so he can call Peru.
5. I called _____ _____ to get the pizzeria's phone number.
6. He left her six messages, but she never _____ his calls.
7. If she's not at home, try to call her on her _____ phone.
8. Could you _____ _____ for just a minute? I'll see if she's in.
9. We'd all like to hear what you have to say, so I'm going to put you on _____ _____.
10. Jordan checks his _____ _____ every morning when he gets in to the office.
11. Cindy likes to read _____ _____ that her friends send her on her cell phone.
12. All of the board members will be on the _____ _____ next week.
13. I'm calling in _____ to the proposal you sent me.
14. If you don't want to bring a cell phone, make sure you take your _____ with you in case someone needs to reach you.

10C TAKE A CLOSER LOOK

USING *CAN* AND *MAY*

In the first dialogue, you hear Anna ask, *"May I ask who's calling?"* *Can* and *may* have similar meanings in English, and the rules for using them are often relaxed in conversation. Let's listen to a few examples. Note that the first two sentences are both correct.

🎧 *Excuse me, can I use your phone?*
Excuse me, may I use your phone?
Who's calling?
May I ask who's calling?
How old are you?
May I ask how old you are?

📖 If you want to be very correct, you should always use *may* in polite requests:

May I offer you a drink?
May I sit down here?
May I call you tomorrow evening?
May I ask who's on the line?

Can should be used only to show physical or other actual capability. It is very common to hear *can* used colloquially to mean the same thing as *may*, but if you want to be very correct, you will use *may* for polite requests, and *can* to show capability. Take a close look at these pairs of sentences.

I can speak French, Spanish, and English.
May I speak with you?
I can come to the party tomorrow if I'm feeling better.
May I come with a friend?
I can buy dinner tonight—I just got paid!
May I buy you dinner tonight?

PRACTICE: USING *CAN* AND *MAY*
Complete each of the following sentences with *can* or *may*. For this exercise, use the "very correct" rule.

1. _____ I please go the bathroom?
2. _____ you carry all of those suitcases by yourself?
3. _____ I help you?
4. John's strong; he _____ help you lift those boxes.
5. Jennifer _____ afford a much bigger apartment. She earns a lot of money.
6. No, you _____ not eat dinner in bed, children!
7. _____ I interrupt for a second?
8. _____ I take your coat?
9. _____ they finish the work by themselves?
10. Geoffrey _____ not make it to the reception tonight.

EACH OTHER AND ONE ANOTHER

In the second dialogue, you listened as Mr. Shapiro and Mr. Tirelli tried to contact each other. Let's take a moment and review the rules of using *each other* and *one another*. It's very simple, actually. Use *each other* when you're talking about two people. Use *one another* when you're talking about three or more people.

Peter and John phoned each other last night.
Mary and Suzanne send a lot of e-mails to each other.
The members of the committee spoke to one another for hours.
John, Harry, and Mike met one another after work for drinks last night.

PRACTICE: EACH OTHER AND ONE ANOTHER

Choose *each other* or *one another* to complete each of the following sentences.

1. Mr. and Mrs. Jensen see _____ _____ every day for lunch.
2. The three children bought _____ _____ birthday gifts.
3. All of the players on the basketball team have known _____ _____ for years.
4. Sarah and Tracy tell _____ _____ their secrets.
5. My sister and I talk to _____ _____ at least twice a month.
6. All of the department heads meet with _____ _____ once a month.
7. Linda and Sally don't speak to _____ _____.
8. You and I haven't seen _____ _____ in months!
9. Gary, Joe, and Paul met _____ _____ at a party two years ago.
10. Dora and her mother send _____ _____ a lot of e-mail.

THE PAST PERFECT TENSE

We've already taken a closer look at two ways to talk about actions in the past, with a review of the present perfect tense (*have/has gone*) and the past tense (*went*). Now let's look at the past perfect tense (*had gone*).

The past perfect tense is formed with *had* plus a past participle. (If you'd like to review irregular past participles, you can turn back to Lesson 7 at any time and take another look at the section on the present perfect tense.) This tense is used to talk about something that happened in the past *before* another action. You use it when you want to stress the order or sequence of actions. Let's look at some examples:

*I'm sorry I missed your phone call, but I **had** already **left** when you called.*
*John **had** already **eaten** when Mary got home.*
*We **had** just **arrived** at the airport when it started to rain.*
*You went to Amsterdam again on vacation? But you'**d** already **gone** there five times!*
*Bill **had studied** two other languages before he started studying German.*

PRACTICE: THE PAST PERFECT TENSE

Combine each of the following pairs of sentences using the past perfect tense and the cues provided.

1. You left. I woke up at 7:30. (already . . . when)
2. The plane took off. We got to the airport. (just . . . when)
3. Gary finished the job. Tracy walked into the office. (already . . . before)
4. I moved to Boston. Marsha moved to Miami. (. . . before)
5. Adrian finished the book. Susan started it. (already . . . before)
6. Did you hear the news? Did you see it on T.V.? (already . . . when)
7. Richard drank two cups of coffee. The waitress offered him a third. (already . . . when)
8. We sold the car. The man called and asked about it. (before)

10D LISTENING EXERCISE

🎧 Listen to each of the recorded sentences and rephrase them as polite requests using the cues provided.

1. *I want to use your pen.* (may)
2. *What is this about?* (may I ask)
3. *I want to take you to dinner tonight.* (can)
4. *I want to help you.* (can)
5. *When will he be back?* (may I ask)

ANSWER KEY—PRACTICE SECTIONS

VOCABULARY

1. Call waiting	5. directory	8. hold on	12. conference call
2. call in	9. speaker phone		13. reference
3. message	6. returned	10. voice mail	14. beeper
4. calling card	7. cell	11. text messages	

USING CAN AND MAY

1. May	4. can	7. May	9. Can
2. Can	5. Can	8. May	10. can
3. May	6. may		

EACH OTHER AND ONE ANOTHER

1. each other	4. each other	7. each other	9. one another
2. one another	5. each other	8. each other	10. each other
3. one another	6. one another		

THE PAST PERFECT TENSE

1. You had already left when I woke up at 7:30.
2. The plane had just taken off when we got to the airport.
3. Gary had already finished the job before Tracy walked into the office.
4. I had moved to Boston before Marsha moved to Miami.
5. Adrian had already finished the book before Susan started it.
6. Had you already heard the news when you saw it on T.V.?
7. Richard had already drunk two cups of coffee when the waitress offered him a third.
8. We had sold the car before the man called an asked about it.

LISTENING EXERCISE

1. May I use your pen?
2. May I ask what this is about?
3. Can I take you to dinner tonight?
4. Can I help you?
5. May I ask when he will be back?

Lesson 11
DINING OUT

Lesson 11 takes you to a restaurant, so as you can imagine you'll hear and review vocabulary associated with restaurants, making reservations, and food in general. Then you'll go back and review how to express preference with *would rather*. You'll also have a chance to review verbs that are followed by gerunds, or the *–ing* form, such as *to enjoy doing something* or *to look forward to seeing someone*.

11A DIALOGUE

A TABLE FOR TWO, PLEASE

Martin and Ewa have made plans to have dinner together. Let's listen in as Martin makes a reservation.

Hostess: *Palace Restaurant.*

Martin: *Hi. I'd like to make dinner reservations for seven-thirty tonight.*

Hostess: *We're all booked at seven-thirty. How about eight or eight-thirty?*

Martin: *Eight o'clock is fine.*

Hostess: *For how many?*

Martin: *There will be two of us.*

Hostess: *What's your name and number, please?*

Martin: *Stevens. My number is 866-7152.*

Hostess: *So, that's a table for two at 8:00 P.M. We look forward to seeing you, Mr. Stevens.*

(AT THE RESTAURANT)

Waiter: *We have a few specials on the menu this evening. First there's a lovely pepper steak served with beans and potatoes. And we have a delicious shrimp dish in a garlic sauce served over rice.*

Ewa: *Which one would you recommend?*

Waiter: *I think the steak is the best thing on the menu.*

Ewa: *OK, I'll have that then.*

Waiter: *How would you like your steak?*

Ewa: *Medium rare.*

Waiter: *Anything to drink?*

Ewa: *What kind of beer do you have on tap?*

Waiter: *Miller, Bud, and Coors.*

Ewa: *A Bud, please.*

Waiter: *Sure.*

Ewa: *Actually, I'd rather have carrots than beans with my steak.*

Waiter: *I'll check with the chef, but I'm sure that won't be a problem.*

Ewa: *Great.*

(A LITTLE WHILE LATER)

Waiter: *Would you like some coffee or dessert?*

Martin: *I could go for some coffee. And you?*

Ewa: *Nothing for me, thanks.*

Waiter: *American coffee, sir?*

Martin: *I'd rather have a cappuccino. And the check, please.*

Waiter: *Right away.*

Now listen to the dialogue again. This time, repeat after the native speakers in the pauses provided.

 11B   WORDS IN ACTION

📖 *reservation*
If you call to get a reservation, you won't have to wait for a table at the restaurant.

reserve
Call ahead to reserve a table; the restaurant is popular.

booked
Sorry, we have no more rooms available. We're booked.

book
I need to book my plane tickets to Vancouver.

specials
Always ask for specials. They're usually the best dishes at a restaurant.

wine list
Would you like to see our wine list?

recommend
I recommend the garlic chicken. He recommended that I take the bus instead of the subway.

on tap
We have only Coors on tap, but we have a variety of bottled beer.

main course
They always have meat, fish, and vegetarian main courses.

appetizer (starter)
Are you going to order an appetizer (a starter) before the main course?

check
Excuse me, can we have the check, please?
I'm not sure if Mr. Wesley is in, but I'll check with his assistant.

go for
I'm hungry! I could really go for some lunch.
Sarah said she could go for a movie tonight.

🎧 Now turn on the recordings and listen to the vocabulary in bold. Repeat each word or expression, and the example sentence, in the pauses provided.

📖 PRACTICE: VOCABULARY

reservation	specials	main course
reserves	wine list	appetizer
booked	recommend	check
book	on tap	go for

1. I don't want bottled beer, so I'll see what they have _____ _____.
2. Would you like to hear the _____ we have available tonight?
3. Hello, I'd like to _____ a ticket from New York to Miami.
4. I'm sorry, we have no tables tonight; we're all _____.
5. Could we have the _____? We're ready to leave.
6. I'd like a glass of chardonnay. Is there anything good on the _____ _____?
7. She always calls and makes a _____ for lunch.
8. I feel like a snack. I could really _____ _____ some potato chips.
9. I always get spring rolls as an _____ at the Thai restaurant.
10. I'm not familiar with any of this food. What do you _____?
11. I loved the starters and the dessert, but the _____ _____ was disappointing.
12. My assistant _____ all of my hotel rooms for me when I have to travel.

11C TAKE A CLOSER LOOK

EXPRESSING PREFERENCE WITH *WOULD RATHER*

A very common way of expressing preference in English is with the construction *would rather*. After *would rather*, you can use . . .

. . . a verb:

I'd rather stay.

. . . or a negative verb:

I'd rather not stay.

. . . or even a complete idea:

I'd rather we stay for a little longer.

You can also add what you don't prefer after the word *than*:

I'd rather we stay for a little longer than go right now.

Let's listen to several more examples of this.

🎧 ***Would you like coffee?***
I'd rather have tea than coffee.

Would you like chicken?
I'd rather have beef than chicken.
I'd rather have beef.
I'd rather not talk about it.
I'd rather not eat in this restaurant.
Does she want to leave now?
She'd rather stay.
Will you call him now?
I'd rather not call him at all.
Should I ask for the check now?
I'd rather you ask for the check later.

PRACTICE: EXPRESSING PREFERENCE WITH *WOULD RATHER*

Answer each of the following questions using *would rather* and the clues provided. For example, if you see "*Would you like some coffee? (tea)*" you should answer "*I'd rather have some tea.*" Use contractions in your answer.

1.   Do you want to go to the movies tonight? (go to a restaurant)
2.   Would you like to sit in the front? (in the back)
3.   Does he want to have Italian tonight? (Indian)
4.   Would you like to get a cat? (dog)
5.   Do they want us to go out? (we stay home)
6.   Do you want to sit in a booth? (at a table)
7.   Would they like to go hiking? (swimming)
8.   Do you want to stay at this hotel? (the other one)

VERBS FOLLOWED BY THE GERUND

We've already talked a lot about the *-ing* form of the verb in English. As you know, it's important for many verb tenses: *I am **studying**, you were **talking**, he has been **working** . . .* But the same forms are also sometimes used as nouns, even though they look like verbs. For example:

***Studying** is important if you want to get good grades.*
***Talking** during a performance is rude!*
*She says she likes **working**, but I don't believe her.*

Technically, when the *-ing* form is used as a noun, it's called a gerund. The tricky thing about English is to know when you should use the gerund. Did you notice that in the dialogue the hostess said, "*We look forward to seeing you, Mr. Stevens*"? That's because *to look forward to* is one of those expressions that is followed by the gerund. Let's review several other common expressions.

We'll start with the harder ones. Many verbs in English are followed first by a preposition (*to, for, in*) and then by a gerund. *To look forward to* is one of them.

get used to
Molly can't **get used to living** without her dog; she's lonely.

agree on
We **agreed on trying** that new Vietnamese restaurant.

apologize for
John **apologized for making** such a mess.

ask about
We **asked about getting** a membership at the club.

believe in
I **believe in doing** a thorough job!

blame for
He got **blamed for breaking** the computer.

care about
I don't **care about missing** the movie; I've seen it.

complain about
She **complained about getting** cold soup.

decide on
They **decided on driving** to work instead of taking the train.

help with
They **helped with moving** the furniture.

keep on
You **keep on asking** me, but I keep on saying the same thing—no!

look forward to
We **look forward to going** on vacation.

succeed in
They've **succeeded in making** everyone angry.

talk about
We **talk about moving**, but I'm not sure if we'll do it.

be no point in
There's no point in arguing; you'll never convince her.

think about
I will **think about getting** a new job.

worry about
Don't **worry about getting** in trouble; they'll never find out!

Now let's take a look at something a bit easier—verbs that are just followed directly by a gerund.

admit
He **admitted stealing** the money.

anticipate
I **anticipate having** trouble.

appreciate
They **appreciate** our **helping** them move.

avoid
We **avoided driving** through the center of town.

consider
I **considered applying** for a job with that company.

delay
She **delayed telling** me the truth.

deny
He **denied taking** the wallet.

discuss
Joanne and Ray **discussed buying** a new car.

dislike
I **dislike going** to the movies.

enjoy
Does Samantha **enjoy cooking** dinner for so many people?

feel like
We **feel like staying** home tonight and **watching** television.

finish
They **finished taking** the test an hour ago.

imagine
I can't **imagine living** in such a big house!

mind
Do you **mind waiting** in the car?

quit
They've finally **quit smoking**.

recall
I don't **recall telling** you that!

recommend
Would you **recommend taking** the bus or the train?

regret
Keith **regrets telling** you about their conversation.

resent
She **resents having** to live here.

risk
You **risk making** everyone mad.

suggest
I **suggested going** to a restaurant last night.

tolerate
Paul can't **tolerate walking** in the cold.

PRACTICE: VERBS FOLLOWED BY THE GERUND 1
Complete each of the following sentences with the correct preposition.

1. When I was at the bank I asked _____ opening an account.
2. Don't blame me _____ causing this mess!
3. We really look forward _____ seeing you over the holidays!
4. We've finally decided _____ staying here instead of moving.
5. I haven't succeeded _____ convincing her.
6. There's no point _____ waiting any more—she's not coming.
7. The neighbors complained _____ being able to hear our party last night.
8. You need to apologize _____ saying such cruel things.

PRACTICE: VERBS FOLLOWED BY THE GERUND 2
Complete each of the following sentences with one of the following verbs:

discuss, finish, recommend, regret, dislike, tolerate, risk, consider.

1. Would you _____ taking the train into the city?
2. Yes, I'll _____ speaking to a lawyer. That's a good idea.
3. She can't _____ sitting next to smokers at a restaurant.
4. Did you _____ having that professor for your course, or was he okay?
5. Well, we did _____ buying a new car, but in the end we decided on a used car.
6. When will you _____ writing the report? It's due today.
7. That was an awful vacation! I _____ paying all of that money!
8. Don't _____ putting all of your money into those stocks! You could lose everything.

PRACTICE: VERBS FOLLOWED BY THE GERUND 3
Use the words and phrases below to make complete sentences. Don't forget to add *-ing* or a preposition where you have to.

1. We succeeded // get // their approval for the new proposal.
2. My colleagues suggested // stay // at this hotel.
3. Cindy regrets // not // come // with us to the restaurant.

4. You should avoid // take // Route 80 at this time of the day.
5. Jordan apologized // not // come // to the party.
6. We can't get used // live // in such a small apartment.
7. Diane doesn't worry // get // to work late.
8. Peter doesn't mind // wait // for us.
9. My sister delayed // come // to visit us.
10. I don't recall // be // here before.
11. What do you think // go // camping instead?
12. Do you believe // do // the best job you can?

11D LISTENING EXERCISE

🎧 Listen to the recorded questions and answer using *rather* and the clues provided.

1. ***Would you like some wine?*** (beer)
2. ***Would you like me to call you tomorrow?*** (tonight)
3. ***Do you want to eat at home?*** (not at all)
4. ***Should we go now?*** (wait)
5. ***Do you want to discuss this now?*** (not at all)

ANSWER KEY—PRACTICE SECTIONS

VOCABULARY

1. on tap	4. booked	7. reservation	10. recommend
2. specials	5. check	8. go for	11. main course
3. book	6. wine list	9. appetizer	12. reserves

EXPRESSING PREFERENCE WITH WOULD RATHER

1. I'd rather go to a restaurant tonight.
2. I'd rather sit in the back.
3. He'd rather have Indian tonight.
4. I'd rather get a dog.
5. They'd rather we stay home.
6. I'd rather sit at a table.
7. They'd rather go swimming.
8. I'd rather stay at the other one.

VERBS FOLLOWED BY THE GERUND 1

1. about	3. to	5. in	7. about
2. for	4. on	6. in	8. for

VERBS FOLLOWED BY THE GERUND 2

1. recommend	3. tolerate	5. discuss	7. regret
2. consider	4. dislike	6. finish	8. risk

VERBS FOLLOWED BY THE GERUND 3

1. We succeeded in getting their approval for the new proposal.
2. My colleagues suggested staying at this hotel.
3. Cindy regrets not coming with us to the restaurant.
4. You should avoid taking Route 80 at this time of the day.
5. Jordan apologized for not coming to the party.
6. We can't get used to living in such a small apartment.
7. Diane doesn't worry about getting to work late.
8. Peter doesn't mind waiting for us.
9. My sister delayed coming to visit us.
10. I don't recall being here before.
11. What do you think about going camping instead?
12. Do you believe in doing the best job you can?

LISTENING EXERCISE

1. I'd rather have beer.
2. I'd rather you call me tonight.
3. I'd rather not eat at all.
4. I'd rather we wait.
5. I'd rather not discuss this at all.

Lesson 12

AT THE POST OFFICE

Lesson 12 takes you to a post office, where you'll of course hear a lot of vocabulary used for mailing letters and packages. But you'll also review essential vocabulary for all of the other kinds of mail that we have today, such as e-mail. After that you'll review the use of *a, an, each,* and *per* in expressions of price or frequency, as in *$6.00 a pack* or *once each year*. Finally, you'll take a closer look at verbs that are followed by infinitives instead of gerunds.

12A DIALOGUE

ONE MORE THING . . .
Let's listen as Mary Higgins checks off a number of things on her to-do list at the post office.

Mary Higgins: *Good morning. I'd like ten airmail stamps.*
Mail Clerk: *That's 50 cents a stamp. Anything else?*
Mary Higgins: *Yes, this letter needs to go by registered mail.*
Mail Clerk: *Where's it going?*
Mary Higgins: *To the New York State Department of Taxation.*
Mail Clerk: *You'll want to make sure that gets there on time! Fill out this form and sign at the bottom.*
Mary Higgins: *Here you go.*
Mail Clerk: *OK, that's 29 cents for the stamp, and $2.00 to send it by registered mail. Is that it?*
Mary Higgins: *Not quite. The next thing on my list is a money order.*
Mail Clerk: *Let me fill out the order form. Who is the addressee?*
Mary Higgins: *English Language Textbooks.*
Mail Clerk: *And the address?*
Mary Higgins: *125 Chambers Street, Santa Monica, California, 90401.*
Mail Clerk: *And the amount of the money order?*
Mary Higgins: *$15.75.*
Mail Clerk: *We charge $1.50 per money order, so that'll be $17.25 total. Anything else on that list of yours?*
Mary Higgins: *One more thing. This letter is urgent.*
Mail Clerk: *If you send it express mail, it'll be $9.75 for the first twelve ounces.*
Mary Higgins: *Fine. It's only a letter; it doesn't weigh much.*
Mail Clerk: *Fill out the form, and put the letter inside this express mail envelope.*
Mary Higgins: *Thanks. That's all.*
Mail Clerk: *Now, here's the bad news: your total is $34.29!*

Now listen to the dialogue a second time and repeat after the native speakers in the pauses provided.

12B WORDS IN ACTION

clerk
Frank works as a clerk in a supermarket.
If you have any questions about the hotel, see the desk clerk.

airmail stamps
You need airmail stamps to send letters overseas.

overnight
This package needs to get to San Francisco tomorrow, so I'll send it by overnight delivery.
If the client needs it by tomorrow, you'd better overnight it.

registered mail
When you send a letter via registered mail, the addressee must sign for it.

ship
I ordered a book on the Internet, but it takes three days for them to ship it to me.

shipping
How much does the shipping cost?

money order
They don't take checks, cash, or credit cards; they only accept money orders.

urgent
It's urgent; it must be there by 10:00 A.M. tomorrow.

express mail
Express mail is the fastest way to send a letter.

e-mail
If you want to send me a message, e-mail it. Letters take too long. E-mail me tonight!

snail mail
Since regular mail is much slower than e-mail, some people call it "snail mail."

🎧 Now turn on the recordings and listen to the vocabulary in bold. Repeat each word or expression, and the example sentence, in the pauses provided.

PRACTICE: VOCABULARY

📖
clerk	shipping	express mail
airmail stamps	money order	e-mail
overnight	urgent	snail mail
registered mail		

1.   It's cheaper to buy that online, but the _____ can be expensive.
2.   I waited in line at the post office until the _____ called "next!"
3.   Don't send that message by _____ _____! It'll take forever!
4.   If you need to send a letter quickly, use _____ _____.
5.   This package is _____. It's got some very important documents that need to be in London quickly.

6. I wanted to send a letter to my friend in Lebanon, but I didn't have any
   _____ _____. I have to go the post office to get some.

7. If those documents are very important, you should send them _____
   _____.

8. It's very expensive to _____ letters and packages to Tokyo, but they
   need this package tomorrow.

9. Please don't _____ me jokes or funny articles at work. I'm too busy!

10. If they won't take a check or credit card, give them a _____ _____.

12C TAKE A CLOSER LOOK

USING A, AN, PER, AND EACH

In the dialogue you heard the clerk listing the prices of various items: *50
cents a stamp, $1.50 per money order*. Did you notice how *a* and *per* were
used? Listen to a few more examples of this useful construction.

That's 29 cents a stamp.
She goes to the post office once a month.
The speed limit is 55 miles an hour.
You should study English at least twice each week.
The potatoes are $1.50 per kilo.
The stamps? They're 29 cents each.

You can use *a, an, per,* and *each* to list prices or to talk about how often
something happens in a given time period. They can more or less be used
interchangeably. Here are some more examples:

She walks to work twice a week./She walks to work twice each week.
*That column appears once an issue in that magazine./That column appears
once per issue in that magazine.*
Those candies cost $5.00 per pound./Those candies cost $5.00 a pound.
*The store was giving out free gifts, one-per-customer./The store was giving
out free gifts, one-to-a-customer.*
*She lives on the top floor of the building and climbs the stairs many times
each day./She lives on the top floor of the building and climbs the stairs
many times a day.*

PRACTICE: USING A, AN, PER, AND EACH

Answer each of the following questions using the clues provided.

1. How many times a week do you go out to dinner? (three)
2. How much do the roses cost? ($25 a dozen)
3. How often does he work? (4 days per week)
4. How often does he talk to his sister each month? (once)
5. How much do the pens cost? ($1.00 each)
6. How fast were you driving? (65 miles per hour)

VERBS FOLLOWED BY THE INFINITIVE

In Lesson 11 we reviewed some common verbs that are followed by the gerund, such as *complain about **doing** something*, or *regret **doing** something*. But did you notice in the dialogue that Mary Higgins said *"this letter needs **to go** by registered mail?"* *Need* is an example of a verb that is followed by the infinitive, or the "to" form of the verb. Just like verbs followed by gerunds, there are many verbs that are followed by the infinitive. And you just need to memorize them!

But let's make this easy. Here's a list of the most common and important verbs that are followed by the infinitive:

agree
We **agreed to meet** and speak about the matter later.

afford
I can't **afford to go** to the Caribbean this year.

appear
She **appears to be** angry about something.

arrange
Will you **arrange to pick** them up at the airport?

ask
He **asked to be told** when dinner was ready.

care
I don't **care to speak** to him about it.

choose
John **chose to go** there on his own.

dare
Do you **dare to refuse** their request?

decide
When did you **decide to leave** your job?

demand
Karin **demands to know** the truth!

deserve
He doesn't **deserve to come** on vacation with us.

expect
Do you **expect to leave** shortly?

fail
Jennifer **failed to submit** the application on time.

happen
Would you **happen to know** what time it is?

have
They don't **have to take** the test until next week.

hope
I **hope to finish** up here by 6:00.

intend
She **intends to leave** him a message as soon as she knows.

learn
How did you **learn to dance** like that?

manage
I **managed to leave** the house without being seen.

need
We really **need to talk**.

offer
Will **offered to help** us move.

plan
Lucian **plans to take** a sick day tomorrow.

prepare
Have you **prepared to go** on your trip yet?

pretend
The children **pretended to be** on a spaceship.

promise
She **promised to do** all of her homework before going out.

refuse
I **refuse to let** it bother me!

seem
You **seem to be** upset about something.

wait
I can't **wait to get** to the beach!

want
Do you **want to have** dinner with us this weekend?

PRACTICE: VERBS FOLLOWED BY THE INFINITIVE
Answer each of the following questions using the clues provided.

1. What did her daughter refuse to do? (eat her dinner)
2. What did he promise his wife? (be home early)
3. What do you want to do? (I, go to Italy on vacation)
4. What did you learn at cooking class tonight? (We, make pie crust)
5. What did Rick demand? (know the truth)

6. What did Sarah and Rebecca choose to do? (stay home and watch T.V.)
7. What can't you wait to do? (I, leave on my trip)
8. What can't they afford to do? (buy a new apartment now)

12D LISTENING EXERCISE

🎧 Listen to the following questions, and answer them using *a* and the clue provided:

1. *How much are these stamps?* (50 cents)
2. *In a week, how often do you write letters?* (once)
3. *How much is a dozen of these roses?* ($10.00)
4. *In a week, how often do you study English?* (twice)

ANSWER KEY—PRACTICE SECTIONS

VOCABULARY

1. shipping
2. clerk
3. snail mail
4. express mail
5. urgent
6. airmail stamps
7. certified mail
8. overnight
9. e-mail
10. money order

USING *A, AN, PER* AND *EACH*

1. I go out to dinner three times a week.
2. The roses cost $25.00 a dozen.
3. He works four days per week.
4. He talks to his sister once each month.
5. The pens cost $1.00 each.
6. I was driving 65 miles per hour.

VERBS FOLLOWED BY THE INFINITIVE

1. Her daughter refused to eat her dinner.
2. He promised his wife to be home early.
3. I want to go to Italy on vacation.
4. We learned to make pie crust at cooking class tonight.
5. Rick demanded to know the truth.
6. Sarah and Rebecca chose to stay home and watch T.V.
7. I can't wait to leave on my trip.
8. They can't afford to buy a new apartment now.

LISTENING EXERCISE

1. They're 50 cents a stamp.
2. I write letters once a week.
3. They're $10.00 a dozen.
4. I study English twice a week.

Lesson 13
AT THE DOCTOR'S OFFICE

In Lesson 13 you'll go to the doctor's office. You'll listen in as a patient makes an appointment and then goes to see her doctor, so naturally you'll hear a lot of vocabulary useful for talking about health and healthcare. Then you'll review the uses of the word *self* in such expressions as *to hurt oneself* or *to do something oneself*. Finally, you'll compare the past tense, the present perfect tense, and the present perfect continuous tense, or *did, has done,* and *has been doing*.

13A **DIALOGUE**

IS IT AN EMERGENCY?

Shirley needs to make an appointment to see her doctor right away. Let's listen in as she speaks to the receptionist on the telephone, and then a little while later during her appointment.

Shirley: *I'd like to make an appointment to see Dr. Lang.*

Receptionist: *Is it an emergency?*

Shirley: *Yes, I have an infected wound.*

Receptionist: *In that case, how about this afternoon at three?*

Shirley: *Fine. My name is Shirley Baker.*

Receptionist: *Have you been here before?*

Shirley: *No.*

Receptionist: *Who referred you to us?*

Shirley: *My neighbor, Vera Dong.*
(A LITTLE LATER)

Shirley: *I'm here to see Dr. Lang.*

Receptionist: *Your name?*

Shirley: *Shirley Baker.*

Receptionist: *Ah, yes. Please fill out this form, with your name, address, and phone number. Do you have health insurance?*

Shirley: *No. Will that be a problem?*

Receptionist: *I don't think so. Stay here. Dr. Lang will be right with you.*
(A MOMENT LATER)

Dr. Lang: *What seems to be the problem?*

Shirley: *Well, I cut myself with a sharp knife the other day, and now my hand is swollen. It seems to be infected.*

Dr. Lang: *When did this happen?*

Shirley: *Last Saturday.*

Dr. Lang: *Could you roll up your sleeve? Does it hurt when I press here?*

Shirley: *A little bit.*

Dr. Lang: *Have you been taking any medication?*

Shirley: *No.*

Dr. Lang: *Do you have a fever?*

Shirley: *No, I don't think so.*

Dr. Lang: *I'll give you a prescription that'll get rid of the infection quickly.*

Shirley: *Thank you, Doctor.*

Now listen to the dialogue again. This time, repeat after the native speakers in the pauses provided.

13B WORDS IN ACTION

check-up
I scheduled my yearly check-up with my doctor for next week.

wound
That's not a minor cut—that's a serious wound! We should go to the hospital.

swollen
My feet are so swollen that my shoes don't fit.

medical benefits
My company offers good medical benefits, so I pay very little for doctor's visits.

co-payment
Every time I go to the doctor's office I have to pay a small co-payment for the visit.

insurance
–Does Dr. Stern accept my insurance? –Yes, she accepts all major insurance plans.

infection
I have an ear infection.

patient
All of Dr. Guthrie's patients like him very much.

medication
Are you taking any pills? Are you on any medication?

refer
My doctor referred me to a specialist.
My brother-in-law referred me to his doctor because he's very happy with her.

temperature
Wow, your temperature is 104! You'd better hurry to the hospital.

bandage
After he cleaned my wounds, the nurse bandaged my arm.
Put a bandage on that cut or you'll get an infection!

allergic
Are you allergic to any medications?

ointment
She put antibacterial ointment on the cut so it healed faster.

emergency
If there is an emergency, dial 911.

Now turn on the recordings and repeat each word or expression in bold, along with the example sentence, in the pauses provided.

PRACTICE: VOCABULARY

check-up	insurance	temperature
wound	infection	bandages
swollen	patients	allergic
medical benefits	medication	ointment
co-payment	refer	emergency

1. Make sure that the doctor knows if you're _____ to penicillin.
2. If you don't clean and take care of that cut, you'll get an _____.
3. Every year I go to my doctor for an annual _____.
4. It's an _____! I need to see a doctor right away.
5. My ankle hurts and is very _____; I must have sprained it.
6. My son gets a very high _____ when he's sick.
7. Are you on any _____ for your allergies?
8. Her company doesn't offer any _____ _____, unfortunately, so she's cautious about going to the doctor.
9. My _____ covered most of the hospital costs, buy I had to pay some.
10. You should put some antibacterial _____ on your cut.
11. Could you _____ me to a doctor who specializes in allergies?
12. She accidentally cut herself with a knife and got a bad _____.
13. The nurse changed the _____ I had on my arm.
14. That's one of Dr. Stevenson's _____.
15. Under most medical insurance plans you have to pay a small _____ when you go to the doctor's office.

13C TAKE A CLOSER LOOK

USES OF SELF
Turn on the CD and listen to the following example sentences:

🎧 *The mother washed the children.*
The children washed themselves.
Tom and Ann blamed themselves for the accident.
Tom and Ann blamed each other for the accident.
The nurse answered the doctor's phone.
The doctor answered the phone himself.

Did you notice the form of *self* in at least one sentence in each pair of examples? Let's look at the first pair first.

In the statement *The mother washed the children* you know that the mother did the action of washing—she washed the children. But the statement *The children washed themselves* is different. It's called reflexive, because the action (washing) reflects back on the people doing the action (the children). In the dialogue you heard Shirley use the same construction when she said *I cut myself with a sharp knife.* She didn't cut anyone else, and no one cut her—she cut herself.

It's easy to make a verb reflexive in English. Just use a reflexive pronoun: *myself, yourself, himself, herself, itself, oneself, ourselves, yourselves* (for more than one *you*) and *themselves.* Let's look at some more examples:

I always cut myself shaving!
You gave yourself a birthday present?
He burned himself with a cigarette.
She blamed herself for the accident.
The bird hurt itself when it flew into the window.
One should excuse oneself when one leaves the table.
The mirror was so dirty we couldn't even see ourselves in it.
All of you should listen to yourselves! You sound like fools!
They put themselves in danger by not calling the police.

Now take a look at the second pair from the earlier examples: *Tom and Ann blamed themselves for the accident* and *Tom and Ann blamed each other for the accident.* Can you tell the difference? The first one is reflexive, just like our examples above. Tom and Ann don't blame anyone else but themselves for the accident. But the second example is called reciprocal. That's just a technical way of saying that Tom blamed Ann, and Ann blamed Tom, but Tom and Ann did not blame themselves or anyone else. Notice that the important pronoun here is *each other*, and not *ourselves, yourselves,* or *themselves.*

Let's make this clearer with some more examples:

Jenny and I met each other in the street the other day.
The twins understand each other better than anyone else does.
My parents gave each other anniversary gifts.
If you two kids don't stop hitting each other, you're not getting any dessert!

Now let's take a look at one last use of *self.* Normally in a doctor's office you wouldn't expect the doctor to answer the phone. But the very last example was *The doctor answered the phone himself.* Here *himself* isn't reflexive, but instead it stresses that the doctor (instead of a nurse or a receptionist) did the action (answering the phone). Let's look at some more examples:

–Did the mechanic repair your car? –No, I repaired it myself!
–Did you hire someone to paint the house? –No, we did the painting ourselves.
The little girl was proud that she could tie her shoes herself.
His assistant was out, so Mr. Whitman sent the package himself.

PRACTICE: USES OF *SELF* 1
Fill in the blanks with the correct pronoun.

1. I burned _____ on the stove!
2. Kids, did you wash _____ before dinner?
3. Larry put _____ in harm's way when he rescued the swimmer.
4. Oh, they shouldn't take _____ so seriously!
5. Karin talks to _____ when she types.
6. We only have _____ to thank for this mess!
7. Joshua and Frank treated _____ to good seats at the baseball game.
8. You need to give _____ a break! You've all been working too hard.

PRACTICE: USES OF *SELF* 2
Rewrite the sentences using reflexive pronouns . For example, *John saw Judy in the mirror* would become *John saw himself in the mirror.*

1. Hillary gave Samantha a birthday present.
2. Don gave the kids a bath this morning.
3. Paul hurt Jerry playing football yesterday.
4. I got you into trouble.
5. Karen sees Cindy as a the next director of the department.
6. The kids gave their parents more food.
7. You don't take me seriously!
8. We excused them from the table.

PRACTICE: USES OF *SELF* 3
Rewrite each of the following sentences using *each other*.

1. Jason doesn't like Larry, and Larry doesn't like Jason.
2. Victor gave Brian a CD for his birthday, and Brian gave Victor a CD for his birthday, too.
3. You trust me, and I trust you.
4. Billy, you stop bothering Kevin, and Kevin, you stop bothering Billy!
5. I told you a secret, and you told me a secret.
6. I saw you coming into the office, and you saw me coming into the office.

THE PAST, PRESENT PERFECT, AND PRESENT PERFECT CONTINUOUS TENSES
You've already taken a closer look at each of these tenses separately, and you saw all three of these tenses used in the dialogue: *Have you been here before? I cut myself with a sharp knife the other day. Have you been taking any medication?* Let's take a moment now to sort these tenses out and review exactly how to use them one last time.

The simple past tense, or just the past tense, is the tense you choose when you want to talk about an action that happened in the past. Some verbs are regular (walked, talked, e-mailed, commuted) but many very common ones are irregular (ate, went, slept, spoke). You'll use this tense when you're telling a story about things that happened in the past, when you're talking about history, or when you mention a specific time or date when something happened. Let's see some examples:

I went to the store and bought groceries last night.
Mary left the office at 5:45 today.
They talked for hours on the telephone.
We took a wonderful trip last summer.
The Normans invaded England in 1066.
Kublai Khan became ruler of the Mongol Empire in 1287.
John F. Kennedy was assassinated in 1963.

The present perfect tense, like the past tense, is used to talk about an action that happened in the past, but there are two important differences between the two tenses. The first important difference is that the simple past tense is used if the time frame is finished (last year, last week, yesterday), but the present perfect tense is used if the time frame is not finished (this year, this week, today). The second important difference is that the present perfect tense suggests something more about the present or future because of what has happened in the past. To understand this, take a look at these examples in both the simple past and the present perfect. The notes in parentheses will help you understand why each tense was chosen.

I went to work five days last week. (And last week is finished.)
I have gone to work three days this week. (So far. This week is not finished.)
I've gone to work three days this week. (And I'll most likely go two more times.)

Amrita was in China in 2002. (2002 is finished, so it's just a "historical" fact.)
I've never been to China. (The time frame is my life, which is still unfinished.)
I've never been to China. (But I would really like to go there some day.)

Did you see Richard in the conference room? (You're not in the conference room any more, so that time frame is finished.)
Have you seen Richard? ("Yet" or "this morning" or "today" is understood. It's an unfinished time frame.)
Have you seen Richard? (Because there's something that I want to tell him.)

There are certain words that will often be used with the present perfect tense instead of the past tense if you're talking about a past action. Take a look at these examples with *yet, still, already, ever, never, before,* and *always.*

Have you finished the report yet?
She still hasn't told me whether she wants to come with us.

They've already called three times today.
Have you ever heard of such nonsense?
We have never been here.
Have you been to this restaurant before?
I've always wanted to learn to speak Chinese.

The present perfect continuous tense, as you know, is used to talk about an action that began in the past, but continues up to the present. It may or may not continue on through the future. Remember that *since* and *for* are often used with time phrases in this tense.

The director has been waiting for your phone call since 9:30 this morning.
We've been sitting on the plane for seven hours already!
I've been working here for six years.
Have they been standing there and listening for a long time?
They haven't been speaking to each other since they got here last night.

Note that the present perfect can often be used in cases where the present perfect continuous is correct.

I've worked for this company since 1996.
I've been working for this company since 1996.
We've waited for three hours, and no one is here. Let's go!
We've been waiting for three hours, and no one is here. Let's go!

PRACTICE: THE PAST, PRESENT PERFECT, AND PRESENT PERFECT CONTINUOUS TENSES

Complete each of the following sentences with the correct form of the verb given in parentheses. Choose either the simple past, present perfect, or present perfect continuous tense. (In some cases, there will be two correct answers.)

1. She _____ here twice before. (be)
2. They _____ home at 6:00 last night. (go)
3. She _____ on the project since 7:30 this morning. (work)
4. They _____ the film yet, so they're eager to go to the movies. (not see)
5. Were you speaking? I'm sorry, I _____. (not listen)
6. You want to stop again? We _____ three times already! (stop)
7. You _____ Greek for four years in college? You must speak well! (study)
8. They still _____ up their minds. (not make)
9. We _____ to New York in 1991. (move)
10. The baby _____ for three hours. (sleep)
11. I _____ Mr. Lee yet today. (not see)
12. They _____ the news last night after dinner. (hear)

13D LISTENING EXERCISE

🎧 Listen to the recorded questions and answer them using the cues provided.

1. *Did the nurse fill out the form?* (no, ourselves)
2. *Did you cut Mrs. Roth?* (no, herself)
3. *Did the doctor take your temperature?* (no, myself)
4. *Did the doctor or the nurse take the patient's temperature?* (doctor)
5. *Did you or your assistant write this letter?* (I)
6. *Did you or the Bergers call 911?* (Bergers)

ANSWER KEY—PRACTICE SECTIONS

VOCABULARY

1. allergic	5. swollen	9. insurance	13. bandage
2. infection	6. temperature	10. ointment	14. patients
3. check-up	7. medication	11. refer	15. co-payment
4. emergency	8. medical benefits	12. wound	

PRACTICE: USES OF SELF 1

1. myself	3. himself	5. herself	7. themselves
2. yourselves	4. themselves	6. ourselves	8. yourselves

PRACTICE: USES OF SELF 2

1. Hillary gave herself a birthday present.
2. Don gave himself a bath this morning.
3. Paul hurt himself playing football yesterday.
4. I got myself into trouble.
5. Karen sees herself as a the next director of the department.
6. The kids gave themselves more food.
7. You don't take yourself seriously!
8. We excused ourselves from the table.

PRACTICE: USES OF SELF 3

1. Jason and Larry don't like each other.
2. Victor and Brian gave each other CD's for their birthdays.
3. We trust each other.
4. Billy and Kevin, stop bothering each other!
5. We told each other secrets.
6. We saw each other coming into the office.

PRACTICE: THE PAST, PRESENT PERFECT, AND PRESENT PERFECT CONTINUOUS TENSES

1. has been/was	4. haven't seen	6. have stopped	10. has been
2. went	5. haven't been	7. studied	11. haven't seen
3. has been listening/working/has worked		8. haven't made	12. heard
		9. moved	
	wasn't listening		

LISTENING EXERCISE

1. No, we filled out the form ourselves.
2. No, Mrs. Roth cut herself.
3. No, I took my temperature myself.
4. The doctor took the patient's temperature himself.
5. I wrote this letter myself.
6. The Bergers called 911 themselves.

Lesson 14

AT THE DRUGSTORE

In Lesson 14 you'll listen in as two friends meet each other in a drugstore. You'll review useful vocabulary for things you might buy at a drugstore—medicines, healthcare and beauty products, etc. Then you'll review the many uses of the very handy word *right*, as well as the construction *to have somebody do something* or *to have something done*. Finally, you'll take a closer look at the passive voice.

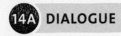 **DIALOGUE**

I HAVEN'T SEEN YOU IN AGES!

June is in the drugstore to have the pharmacist fill a prescription for her. She also needs to pick up a few other items. She's surprised by her friend Barbara, who she hasn't seen in a long time. Let's listen in as they chat, and then as June speaks to the pharmacist.

Barbara:	*Hi, June. I haven't seen you in ages.*
June:	*Barbara, hi, how's it going? I have to pick up some cough medicine for my husband.*
Barbara:	*How about this one here? It'll help him sleep.*
June:	*Let me see. $12.29?! What a rip-off!*
Barbara:	*This one is cherry-flavored and won't cause drowsiness.*
June:	*I'll take that. And I need to get some aspirin, too.*
Barbara:	*I have to get this prescription for my son. He has a cold as well.*
June:	*I'm sorry to hear that. Would you like to get some coffee afterwards and catch up on things?*
Barbara:	*I'd love to, but I promised my son I'd be home right away.*
June:	*Well, maybe some other time. I'll give you a call.*
Barbara:	*Yes, please do. Bye, and give my best to your husband.*
June:	*I will. Catch you later!*
Barbara:	*Excuse me, sir, I have a prescription to fill.*
Pharmacist:	*Would you prefer tablets or liquid form?*
Barbara:	*Tablets, please.*
Pharmacist:	*Here you go. Take them three times a day right after meals.*
Barbara:	*Thanks a lot.*
Pharmacist:	*And remember, there's a refill on this prescription.*

Now listen to the dialogue again and repeat after the native speakers in the pauses provided.

14B WORDS IN ACTION

age
At what age can people vote in the U.S.?
The Earth was very different during the age of dinosaurs.
I haven't been to the beach in ages!

pick up
Could you pick me up at the train station at 8:00?
She went to the store to pick up some orange juice.

prescription
The doctor gave me a prescription for some strong medicine.

over-the-counter
You can buy over-the-counter medicine, such as aspirin, without a prescription.

decongestant
My nose is so stuffy I can hardly breathe! I need a strong decongestant.

cough syrup
You've got a really bad cough! Take some cough syrup!

refill
I've finished all these pills; I have to get a refill.

makeup
Where's the makeup counter?

lotion
If your hands are dry, put some lotion on them.

drowsiness
Since some medicines cause drowsiness, it's best not to drive while taking them.

sleeplessness
If you take a non-drowsy medicine before going to bed, it'll cause sleeplessness.

flavor
Medicines used to taste bad, but now they come in many different flavors such as mint, cherry, and chocolate.

supplement
If you don't get enough vitamin A in your diet, you should take a supplement. You can supplement your high-fiber diet with these fiber pills.

cold
I cough and sneeze all the time; I think I'm catching a cold.

flu
I have a fever and bad congestion, my body aches, and I'm tired all the time. I must have the flu.

generic
The brand-name product is too expensive! Get the generic; it's got the same ingredients.

🎧 Now turn on the recordings and listen to the vocabulary in bold. Repeat each word or expression, and the example sentence, in the pauses provided.

PRACTICE: VOCABULARY

age	refill	flavors
pick up	makeup	supplements
prescription	lotion	cold
over-the-counter	drowsiness	flu
decongestant	sleeplessness	generic
cough syrup		

1. I can't take that medicine before I have to drive because it causes
    _____.
2. It comes in two _____—cherry and grape.
3. Molly ran to the store to _____ _____ some groceries.
4. Wow, you sound stuffed up! Aren't you taking a _____?
5. She's been coughing and sneezing all morning—she must have caught a
    _____.
6. Everyone who has the _____ this year has a high fever, upset stomach,
    body aches, and a terrible cough.
7. Lipstick and eye shadow can be found at the _____ counter.
8. My doctor wrote me a _____ for some allergy medicine.
9. Don't take those pills now—it's late and they'll cause _____.
10. Donna always buys _____ drugs because they cost much less
    money.
11. You're coughing so much today. You should take some _____ _____.
12. If I run out of this medicine, I can get a _____ on the prescription.
13. If you don't get enough iron or calcium, you need to take _____.
14. Tommy is very young, and high fevers are not as serious at his _____.
15. Do I need a prescription for that drug, or is it _____ _____ _____?
16. Denise always puts _____ on her face and neck before bed.

14C TAKE A CLOSER LOOK

THE USES OF *RIGHT*

Right is a very common word in English, and it has quite a few different
uses and meanings. Turn on the CD and listen to the following examples.

I'll be right with you.
He promised to come home right away.
I'll call you right back.
Take these pills right after dinner.
I write with my right hand.
Turn right at the intersection.
Two and two is four. Am I right?
This is not the right time to discuss this.
You have the right to remain silent.

📖 From the first four examples, you can see that *right* can mean *immediately*, as in *right away*, or *right after dinner*, or *come right home*. It can also be a direction (the opposite of *left*) as shown in the second group of examples. It also means the same thing as *correct*, as demonstrated in the third group. And finally, a *right* is something that people have under law, such as the *right* to life, liberty, and the pursuit of happiness.

PRACTICE: THE USES OF *RIGHT*
Rewrite each of the following sentences using the word *right*.

1. A customer service representative will be with you immediately.
2. He's not allowed to say something like that to me!
3. The answer we gave was incorrect.
4. I have to pick my friend up immediately after work.
5. The gas station is not on your left-hand side.

TO HAVE SOMEBODY DO SOMETHING/ TO HAVE SOMETHING DONE

If you look back at the introduction to the dialogue you'll see the sentence *June is in the drugstore to have the pharmacist fill a prescription for her.* Let's take a closer look at that useful construction beginning with the verb *have*.

As you can see, June isn't the person who fills the prescription—the pharmacist does it for her. Technically, this is called a "causative," which is easy to understand, because June *causes* the pharmacist to fill the prescription. There are other causative verbs that we'll take a closer look at later, and they mean slightly different things. But in this case, just remember that *have* means something very close to *ask* or *request*.

I had the waiter bring us another bottle of wine. (I asked him for another bottle.)
She had her neighbor's son paint her house. (She requested that he paint the house.)
Mr. Tanaka had the porter carry his bags up to the room. (The guest asked the porter to carry his bags.)
My boss had her assistant page me. (She requested that her assistant page me.)

All of these examples follow the pattern *to have someone do something.* Notice that you can say the same things with the pattern *to have something done*, especially if you don't know or don't want to mention who exactly is doing the work.

I had another bottle of wine brought to us.
She had her house painted.
Mr. Tanaka had his bags carried up to the room.
My boss had me paged.

Notice that in the first set of examples, the base form of the verb is used—*bring, paint, carry, page*—without *to*. But in the second set of examples, where the person doing the action is not mentioned, the past participle is used—*brought, painted, carried,* and *paged.* If you'd like to review any irregular past participles, you can always turn back to Lesson 7.

PRACTICE: *TO HAVE SOMEBODY DO SOMETHING/ TO HAVE SOMETHING DONE* 1

Rewrite each of the following sentences using the construction *have somebody do something.*

1. My boss asked me to type the letter for him.
2. Sally will ask John to call you when the baby is born.
3. Mrs. Morgan asked the plumber to repair her kitchen sink.
4. I asked my doctor to describe the procedure to me.
5. Kirsten and Bill asked their friend to fix their bikes.
6. The reporter asked the senator to explain his position.

PRACTICE: *TO HAVE SOMEBODY DO SOMETHING/ TO HAVE SOMETHING DONE* 2

Now rewrite each of these sentences, changing *to have somebody do something* to *to have something done.*

1. Jerry has his assistant bring a cup of coffee to him each morning.
2. Henry had his landlord replace the broken stove.
3. I'll have the dry cleaner clean my suit tomorrow.
4. Greg had the waiter take his main course back.
5. The teacher had her students rewrite all the reports.
6. Tom will have the barber trim his hair tomorrow.

THE PASSIVE VOICE

Look again at the introduction to the dialogue. In the third sentence you read that *June is surprised by her friend Barbara.* Now compare these two sentences:

Barbara surprises June at the drugstore.
June is surprised by Barbara at the drugstore.

These two sentences mean the same thing, but the first sentence is *active,* and the second is an example of the *passive* voice. June isn't the one who is doing the surprising. Instead she's "passive"—she *is surprised* by Barbara. Here are a few more examples of active and passive sentences:

ACTIVE: *Authors write books.*
PASSIVE: *Books are written by authors.*

ACTIVE: Room service brings breakfast to the guests every morning.
PASSIVE: Breakfast is brought to the guests every morning by room service.
ACTIVE: John wrote the report at the last minute.
PASSIVE: The report was written at the last minute by John.

As you can see, you form the passive voice with the right tense and form of the verb *to be* and a past participle. If you want to mention who or what is doing the action, just use *by*. But often the passive voice is used when that is not known or is not important. For example:

My car has been stolen!
Many people were hurt in the accident.
The athlete hopes that his record will never be broken.
Violators will be prosecuted to the full extent of the law.

PRACTICE: THE PASSIVE VOICE
Rewrite the following active sentences using the passive construction. Only use the word *by* if it's written in parentheses after the sentence.

1. Somebody took my wallet off my desk.
2. People grow oranges in Florida.
3. A friend of mine made this film three years ago. (by)
4. A drunk driver hit my car this morning. (by)
5. A person is watching us!
6. They produce a lot of excellent wine in California.
7. The cat or the dog has broken Mom's favorite vase! (by)
8. High winds and flooding damage a lot of homes in hurricanes. (by)

14D LISTENING EXERCISE

🎧 Listen to the recorded sentences and restate them using *right*.

1. *The waiter will be with you immediately.*
2. *This is not the correct answer.*
3. *I'll call you back immediately.*
4. *You are allowed to park here.*
5. *Stay here.*

ANSWER KEY—PRACTICE SECTIONS

VOCABULARY

1. drowsiness	5. cold	9. sleeplessness	13. supplements
2. flavors	6. flu	10. generic	14. age
3. pick up	7. makeup	11. cough syrup	15. over-the-counter
4. decongestant	8. prescription	12. refill	16. lotion

THE USES OF RIGHT

1. A customer service representative will be right with you.
2. He doesn't have the right to say something like that to me!
3. The answer we gave was not right.
4. I have to pick my friend up right after work.
5. The gas station is on your right-hand side.

TO HAVE SOMEBODY DO SOMETHING/
TO HAVE SOMETHING DONE 1

1. My boss had me type the letter for him.
2. Sally will have John call you when the baby is born.
3. Mrs. Morgan had the plumber repair her kitchen sink.
4. I had my doctor describe the procedure to me.
5. Kirsten and Bill had their friend fix their bikes.
6. The reporter had the senator explain his position.

TO HAVE SOMEBODY DO SOMETHING/
TO HAVE SOMETHING DONE 2

1. Jerry has a cup of coffee brought to him each morning.
2. Henry had the broken stove replaced.
3. I'll have my suit cleaned tomorrow.
4. Greg had his main course taken back.
5. The teacher had all the reports rewritten.
6. Tom will have his hair trimmed tomorrow.

THE PASSIVE VOICE

1. My wallet was taken off my desk.
2. Oranges are grown in Florida.
3. This film was made by a friend of mine three years ago.
4. My car was hit by a drunk driver this morning.
5. We're being watched!
6. A lot of excellent wine is produced in California.
7. Mom's favorite vase has been broken by the cat or the dog!
8. A lot of homes are damaged in hurricanes by high winds and flooding.

LISTENING EXERCISE

1. The waiter will be right with you.
2. This is not the right answer.
3. I'll call you right back.
4. You have the right to park here.
5. Stay right here.

Lesson 15

IN A DEPARTMENT STORE

In Lesson 15 you'll go shopping for clothes, and you'll hear a lot of vocabulary that will be useful for shopping in all kinds of stores. Then you'll review some of the many uses of the common verb *make*. You'll also take a look at two other causative constructions with *make* and *get*, and two constructions called permissives, formed with *let* and *allow*.

15A   DIALOGUE

DIALOGUE 1: CAN I HELP YOU?

Melissa needs to buy some clothing to wear to a formal party. Let's listen in as she shops.

Salesperson:	*Can I help you?*
Melissa:	*Yes, I'm looking for something to wear to a formal party.*
Salesperson:	*What size do you wear, ma'am?*
Melissa:	*Medium. An eight or a ten.*
Salesperson:	*Let me show you what we have. This dress is very beautiful. It's the latest fashion from Paris. And here's a plaid jacket that matches.*
Melissa:	*Plaid? No way! What about this skirt here?*
Salesperson:	*Good choice. It's made of pure silk. This silk blouse would go with it very well.*
Melissa:	*Let me try it on. Where's the dressing room?*
Salesperson:	*Right over here.*
Melissa:	*Thanks.*
	(A LITTLE LATER)
Salesperson:	*Ah, you look wonderful.*
Melissa:	*Really? Isn't the skirt a bit too long?*
Salesperson:	*We could always make it shorter.*
Melissa:	*That's true. How much is it?*
Salesperson:	*The skirt is $125. And the blouse is on sale for only $69.*
Melissa:	*Okay, I'll take it!*

Now listen to the dialogue again and repeat after the native speakers in the pauses provided.

DIALOGUE 2: I'D LIKE TO RETURN THESE PANTS

Now let's listen as Richard tries to return a pair of pants. Unfortunately, he bought them on sale and isn't able to return them. Still, he tries to get the customer service representative to take them back. Let's see if he's successful.

Richard:	*I bought these pants here the other day, but they're too big. I'd like to return them.*
Customer Service:	*Do you have your receipt with you?*
Richard:	*Sure, here you go.*
Customer Service:	*Sir, these pants were on sale. We don't take returns on sale items.*
Richard:	*How about a store credit?*
Customer Service:	*I'm afraid there are no returns at all on sale merchandise. I'm sorry, there is nothing we can do.*

Listen to the dialogue a second time, and repeat in the pauses provided.

 WORDS IN ACTION

formal
The party is formal, so you should dress up. Don't wear jeans.

casual
When Don goes out with his friends on the weekends, he wears more casual cloths, like jeans and t-shirts.

fashion
Some people care about wearing the latest fashion.

plaid
Most people think of Scotland when they think of plaid.

pattern
I don't like patterns; all of my clothes are solid colors.

print
The little girl is wearing a dress with a floral print—there are little red and yellow flowers on it.

fabric
What fabric is the shirt made of? Is it cotton?

match
You can't wear those shoes with those pants! They don't match at all!

dressing room (also *fitting room*)
You are only allowed four items in the dressing room at a time.

rack
Clothes are hung on racks in clothing stores.

return
These pants are too small; I hope I can return them.

receipt
Always keep the receipts of everything you buy.

cashier
Bring the clothes to the cashier when you want to pay for them.

final sale
This skirt was a final sale; you can't return it.

merchandise
Merchandise is everything that is for sale in a store.

store credit
I can give you a store credit. You can use it to buy any item in this store.

hardware store
I'm going to the hardware store because I need to buy a hammer and some nails.

housewares
I'm looking for paint, new faucets, and a ceiling fan. Where are housewares?

electronics
Go to electronics if you're looking for video games or CD players.

sporting goods
You can buy baseballs, basketballs, soccer balls, and footballs in sporting goods.

🎧 Now turn on the recordings and listen to the vocabulary in bold. Repeat each word or expression, and the example sentence, in the pauses provided.

PRACTICE: VOCABULARY

formal	dressing room	merchandise
casual	rack	store credit
fashion	returned	hardware store
pattern	receipt	housewares
fabrics	cashiers	electronics
match	final sale	sporting goods

1. You don't remember how much you paid? Check the _____.
2. His tie has a _____ of geometrical shapes on it.
3. You're going to a wedding! You need to wear something _____.
4. Jordan's always loved _____, so it's no wonder he works for a designer.
5. He went to the _____ _____ to buy a new screwdriver.
6. Check out the price of these pants! I found them on the sale _____.
7. Courtney can't stand polyester; she only wears natural _____.
8. Sir, you can't take any _____ out of the store unless you've paid for it!
9. If you're looking for camping equipment, you should go to a _____ _____ store.
10. Come out of the _____ _____ and show me how those jeans look!
11. This is a _____ _____; you can't bring these clothes back to the store.
12. Linda decided that she didn't like the blouse, so she _____ it the day after she bought it.
13. Wow—jeans, a tee shirt, sneakers. You sure look _____ today!
14. You should buy the blue blouse; it will _____ the skirt beautifully.
15. You'll find paint in the _____ department.
16. Where are the _____? I want to pay for these clothes.
17. If I can't get my money back, can I at least get _____ _____?
18. Dan loves video games and other _____.

15C TAKE A CLOSER LOOK

USES OF *MAKE*

Make is such a common verb in English that you may not have noticed how many different uses it has. Turn on your CD and listen to a few examples.

🎧 *This company makes silk dresses.*
This blouse is made of cotton.
Your jokes make me laugh.
Don't make me angry.
Hurry up or we won't make the last train.
You'll have to make it home in time for dinner.
What do you make of our new colleague?
What make is your car?

📖 Can you tell how many different ways *make* was used? Let's take a closer look at some of them. Of course it can mean the same thing as *build, create, manufacture, put together* or *construct*:

The kids made a fort out of cushions in the living room.
Birds make nests out of branches and twigs.
She made a dress for herself.
Where do they make that kind of car?

It can also mean *cook*:

What are you making for dinner tonight?
I made risotto last week.

It can mean *earn*:

She makes over $100,000 a year.
They made a lot of money on that deal.

It can mean *be* or *become*:

You'll make an excellent director some day.
I think that the senator would make a great president.

It can mean *catch*:

I didn't make my train this morning, so I'll be in the office late.
Hurry up! We have to make our plane!

It can mean *achieve, win,* or *obtain*:

Terry made first place in the race.
That team will never make the World Series!

It can also mean *judge* or *understand*:

I don't know what to make of that comment.
What did he make of the report?

It can also mean *cause* or *cause to be*:

Onions make me cry!
That film was so scary it made me sleep with the light on.
You're making me angry!

As a noun, it can mean *type* or *brand*:

Please fill in the make and model of your lost car.

Make is also used in several idiomatic expressions, such as *make do* and *make it*:

We can't afford the black leather sofa, so we'll have to make do with the red one.
I'm so glad you could make it to our dinner party!

PRACTICE: USES OF *MAKE*
Rewrite the following sentences using *make*.

1.   What brand of car did you buy?
2.   Don't cause any trouble for me!
3.   I think I'll prepare soup tonight.
4.   You'll be an excellent father some day!
5.   What is that house constructed of?
6.   Don't tease the dog; you'll cause him to be angry.
7.   The kids are building a sand castle on the beach.
8.   He didn't earn as much money as he had thought.

MAKE AND *GET*—MORE CAUSATIVES
In Lesson 14 you took a closer look at the causative constructions *to have someone do something* and *to have something done*. *Make* and *get* are also causatives; in fact, you've already heard an example of *make* used as a causative. Take a look at the third recorded example in the last section: *Your jokes make me laugh.*

To make somebody do something means *to compel, to push*, or *to force*. Often it suggests some kind of power or authority. Here are a few examples:

I wanted to get home early, but my boss made me stay late.
The policeman made Jake pull over because he was speeding.
The snow made us stay inside all day.
His parents made Tim go to his room without dinner.
There's an old saying, "money makes the world go 'round."

In each of these examples above, you can see that there's little or no choice given to the person doing the action. But that's not the case with *to get somebody to do something*. This causative construction suggests convincing, maybe even begging!

I finally got my sister to drive me to the mall after I promised to wash her car.
If you ask very nicely and say please, maybe you'll get me to give you some ice cream.
Jason got me to sell him my old car for $1,000 less than I wanted.
They couldn't get the baby to stop crying.

Notice that you *have* or *make somebody do something*, but you *get somebody* to *do something*. Don't forget that *to*!

PRACTICE: *MAKE* AND *GET*—MORE CAUSATIVES

Complete each of the following sentences with the right form of *make* or *get* in the first blank. Fill in the second blank with *to* only when it's needed.

1. The security guard always _____ us _____ show him our ID cards.
2. Their boss _____ them _____ stay late to finish the reports last night.
3. I tried to _____ my colleague _____ come to dinner with us, but he's busy.
4. The babysitter _____ Jeremy _____ go to bed early because he was misbehaving.
5. Jonathon _____ his friends _____ help him move by buying them dinner.
6. Luckily, Samantha usually _____ someone _____ help her carry her luggage.
7. The twins _____ their parents _____ let them stay out late last weekend.
8. Immigration officials _____ you _____ open your luggage if they suspect you may have something illegal.

LET AND *ALLOW*—PERMISSIVES

Since we've talked so much about causatives, let's take a quick look at permissives, too. The verbs *let* and *allow* are the two most common permissives—they involve giving *permission*. Let's take a look at some examples of how they're used. Just remember that you *let someone do something*, but you *allow someone to do something*.

Harry opened the door and let the dog go outside.
Mr. Walker never allowed his children to watch too much television.
My father never lets me pay for dinner.
Our boss always lets us go home early on Fridays in the summer.

The teacher doesn't allow the students to chew gum in class.
You need to let yourself relax and have a good time!

You can also use the constructions *to let something be done* or *to allow something to be done.* Here are a few examples.

You left the keys in the ignition and the doors unlocked? You let your car be stolen!
Don't allow your mind to be changed.
Our boss never allows a single rule to be broken.
The baby's mother would never let her be harmed.

PRACTICE: *LET* AND *ALLOW*—PERMISSIVES
Rewrite each of the following sentences using the cues provided.

1. The author submitted the manuscript late. (Her editor let . . .)
2. I drove my car with a broken headlight. (The policeman didn't allow . . .)
3. Joe took Larry's new car for a drive. (Larry let . . .)
4. Mrs. Shaw eats too much salt. (Her doctor doesn't let . . .)
5. The dog sleeps in the bed with them. (They let . . .)
6. Her children cross the street alone. (Mrs. Hernandez doesn't allow . . .)
7. We come in to work late every now and then. (Our director allows . . .)
8. The swimmers swim very far out in the ocean. (The lifeguards won't let . . .)

15D LISTENING EXERCISE

🎧 Listen to the recorded sentences and restate them using *make*.

1. *These are leather shoes.*
2. *What do you think of him?*
3. *What are you preparing for dinner?*
4. *What does this company produce?*
5. *Do you think we'll arrive on time?*

ANSWER KEY—PRACTICE SECTIONS

VOCABULARY

1. receipt	6. rack	11. final sale	16. cashiers
2. pattern	7. fabrics	12. returned	17. store credit
3. formal	8. merchandise	13. casual	18. electronics
4. fashion	9. sporting goods	14. match	
5. hardware store	10. dressing room	15. housewares	

USES OF MAKE

1. What make of car did you buy?
2. Don't make any trouble for me!
3. I think I'll make soup tonight.
4. You'll make an excellent father some day!
5. What is that house made of?
6. Don't tease the dog; you'll make him angry.
7. The kids are making a sand castle on the beach.
8. He didn't make as much money as he had thought.

MAKE AND GET—MORE CAUSATIVES

1. The security guard always makes us show him our ID cards.
2. Their boss made them stay late to finish the reports last night.
3. I tried to get my colleague to come to dinner with us, but he's busy.
4. The babysitter made Jeremy go to bed early because he was misbehaving.
5. Jonathon got his friends to help him move by buying them dinner.
6. Luckily, Samantha usually gets someone to help her carry her luggage.
7. The twins got their parents to let them stay out late last weekend.
8. Immigration officials make you open your luggage if they suspect you may have something illegal.

LET AND ALLOW—PERMISSIVES

1. Her editor let the author submit the manuscript late.
2. The policeman didn't allow me to drive my car with a broken headlight.
3. Larry let Joe take his new car for a drive.
4. Her doctor doesn't let Mrs. Shaw eat too much salt.
5. They let the dog sleep in the bed with them.
6. Mrs. Hernandez doesn't allow her children to cross the street alone.
7. Our director allows us to come in to work late every now and then.
8. The lifeguards won't let the swimmers swim very far out in the ocean.

LISTENING EXERCISE

1. These shoes are made of leather.
2. What do you make of him?
3. What are you making for dinner?
4. What does this company make?
5. Do you think we'll make it on time?

Lesson 16

A PARTY

In Lesson 16 you'll listen in as people talk at a party. As you can imagine, you'll hear vocabulary related to family, hobbies, interests, friendships, and other things that people might talk about in social situations. Then you'll review the uses of the word *use*, and you'll also take a closer look at talking about the past with *used to* and *would*. Finally, you'll review using *if* and *would* in the past tense when making conditional or hypothetical statements.

16A DIALOGUE

VERY NICE TO MEET YOU

Let's listen in as three people talk at a party. Listen closely for some of the polite expressions and topics of conversation that you'd want to use in this kind of social situation.

Steven Schwartz:	*Mr. Winter, I'd like you to meet my wife, Maggie.*
Tom Winter:	*Very nice to meet you. This is a wonderful party.*
Maggie Schwartz:	*Nice to meet you. I'm glad you're enjoying yourself.*
Steven Schwartz:	*Would you like something to drink?*
Tom Winter:	*Yes, I'll have a glass of white wine. Thank you.*
Maggie Schwartz:	*There are some hors d'oeuvres over here. Please try some.*
Tom Winter:	*Mmm. They're delicious. What recipe did you use?*
Maggie Schwartz:	*Well, it's a secret! Too bad your wife couldn't join us tonight. I understand she had to leave town on business?*
Tom Winter:	*Yes, unfortunately.*
Maggie Schwartz:	*So that leaves only you to take care of your son?*
Tom Winter:	*We used to have a baby sitter, but now he's old enough to stay home alone.*
Maggie Schwartz:	*How old is he?*
Tom Winter:	*Fourteen.*
Steven Schwartz:	*Where does he go to school?*
Tom Winter:	*He's at Hugh High School in Fairfield.*
Maggie Schwartz:	*What a coincidence. Our youngest goes to school there as well. She'll graduate this spring. Maybe they know each other!*
Tom Winter:	*I doubt it. My son's only in 8th grade. Does your daughter already know what she wants to do after graduation?*
Steven Schwartz:	*She's thinking about going to Boston University.*
Tom Winter:	*Oh, Boston is such a wonderful city for young people. As a matter of fact, I went there just last weekend.*
Maggie Schwartz:	*So did we.*
Tom Winter:	*You're kidding. What did you do there?*
Maggie Schwartz:	*We just stopped for dinner on our way back from a skiing trip.*

Tom Winter:	*How nice! I used to go skiing all the time, but now I just don't seem to find the time. Where did you say you went?*
Steven Schwartz:	*To a small, cozy place in Vermont. You should join us some time.*
Tom Winter:	*I'd love to.*
Maggie Schwartz:	*So tell us, how do you like life in New York?*
Tom Winter:	*It's quite an adjustment. My wife and son are adapting quite well, though.*
Maggie Schwartz:	*And what about you?*
Tom Winter:	*Between you and me, I just can't get used to city life.*

Now listen to the dialogue again. This time, repeat after the native speakers in the pauses provided.

16B WORDS IN ACTION

to enjoy oneself
Are you enjoying yourselves?
We really enjoyed ourselves last night at the party.

stranger
No one at the party knew him—he was a complete stranger.
No, I don't know her. She's a stranger to me.

small talk
Henry hates making small talk about movies or the weather with strangers at parties.

wine
Would you like red or white wine?

hors d'oeuvres
It's not a sit-down dinner party, but there will be hors d'oeuvres to eat if you're hungry.

chat
Let's take a walk and chat; I don't want to sit here and talk about anything serious.

recipe
You have to give me your recipe for these cookies.

acquaintance
I know Olga, but she's not a close friend. She's really more of an acquaintance.

graduation
My son is finishing college this spring; his graduation will be in May.

cozy
Our room was warm and quiet with a great fireplace—it was so cozy!

mutual friend
Joe and Gary both know Peter—he's a mutual friend of theirs.

coincidence
I can't believe you grew up in Vermont as well; what a coincidence.

adjustment
Moving to another country is a big adjustment; everything is different.

to adjust
Nell comes from Arizona, so it's hard for her to adjust to the weather in Boston.

get to know
We should go out to dinner and get to know each other.
We've just started to get to know the area since we moved here two weeks ago.

adapt
It's hard for me to get used to the city, but my wife is adapting well.

pastime
One of my father's favorite pastimes is gardening.

interested in
The Conellys are very interested in sailing.

hobby
Cooking isn't my profession; it's really more of a hobby.

fan
—Are you a baseball fan? —Yes! I really enjoy baseball.

🎧 Now turn on the recordings and listen to the vocabulary in bold. Repeat each word or expression, and the example sentence, in the pauses provided.

PRACTICE: VOCABULARY

📖

enjoy	acquaintance	adjustment
stranger	graduation	to adjust
small talk	cozy	get to know
wine	mutual friend	adapt
hors d'oeuvre	pastimes	interested in
chatted	fan	hobby
recipe	coincidence	

1. Do you know Monica well? Is she a friend or just an _____?
2. I'm a bit hungry. Would anyone else like an _____ _____?
3. This city is so big and impersonal; it's hard to _____ _____ _____ anyone.
4. Did all of you _____ yourselves at the game yesterday?

5. Frank is big _____ of basketball. He never misses a game.
6. If you're invited to a party, it's customary to bring a small gift, such as a bottle of _____.
7. I'm no good at making _____ _____! I don't feel comfortable talking to people I don't know about things such as the weather.
8. Having a baby was a very big _____ for Ron and Diane; their lives changed.
9. I've always thought that stamp collecting is an interesting _____.
10. After _____ Dominic had to move back home and look for a job.
11. We met through a _____ _____, someone we both knew from work.
12. Keith is very _____ _____ languages. He's studying Japanese and Italian now.
13. The ski lodge has very _____ rooms. They're warm, small, and comfortable.
14. –Did you have a serious talk? –No, we just _____ about our lives.
15. One of my favorite _____ is walking along the river in the morning.
16. Laura is finding it hard _____ _____ to life in a new city.
17. Kelly never follows a _____ when she cooks, but her food is delicious.
18. I didn't know a single person at the party; I felt like a total _____.
19. If the company wants to survive, it has to _____ to changing times.
20. You live on 10th Street? What a _____! I live there, too.

16C TAKE A CLOSER LOOK

USES OF USE
Another very common verb in English is *use*. Listen to a few recorded examples:

My mother used butter to make these cookies.
You should use a hammer to hang these pictures.
I used to watch a lot of television, but I don't any more.
As a child, my father used to eat a lot of cookies.
I'm used to working hard; it doesn't bother me any more.
I'm used to this old car; I don't want to sell it.
I'm sure I'll get used to living alone.
Have you gotten used to your new apartment yet?

As you can see, *use* can be a verb meaning *to employ* or *to have for a specific purpose*:

Use a screwdriver to take out those screws! You can't use a hammer for that!
Did you use butter or margarine in those cookies?
I always use a pencil to write; I never use pens.

But there are also a few common and important expressions with *use*.
First of all *used to* can introduce a verb that was a common, regular, or
habitual action in the past. We'll take another look at that later, but here
are few examples:

I used to go camping a lot when I was younger.
The Morgans used to live next door, but they moved away years ago.

This is not the same thing as *to be used to something* or *to be used to
doing something*. These expressions mean that something is familiar
to you.

I moved here two months ago, so I'm not used to the town yet.
Dennis just bought a new car, and he isn't used to driving it yet.
Mrs. Patel is from India, and she's not used to American food yet.

To get used to something is the process of becoming familiar with it.

*I haven't gotten used to living in my new apartment yet. I still haven't
adjusted.*
It takes years to get used to speaking a new language.
It's not easy to get used to a new country.

PRACTICE: USES OF *USE*
Complete each of the following sentences.

1. Sandra _____ (used/used to) a different kind of laundry detergent.
2. The kids _____ (get/are) not used to waking up so early for school yet.
3. We _____ (used/used to) live in that house over there when I was a kid.
4. Marcia lives in Japan and _____ (isn't/doesn't get) used to the food.
5. Have you _____ (been/gotten) used to working here?
6. We're _____ (using/used to) the conference room for a meeting now.
7. Once you _____ (used to/get used to) living here, you'll feel better.
8. They _____ (used to/are used to) go on vacation every summer.
9. Bill _____ (used to/is used to) a much bigger apartment, but he'll adjust.
10. It takes a long time to _____ (be/get) used to the weather here.

THE PAST WITH *USED TO* AND *WOULD*
As you just saw, *used to* can introduce an action that was habitual,
regular, or customary in the past. Let's take another look at that
construction:

Jim used to share a room with his older brother when he was a boy.
*When they lived in California the Selners used to drive a lot more than they
do now.*
I think it used to snow a lot more when I was a kid.
They used to walk to school every day.

Notice that the question and negative forms of this construction are
use to:

Did you use to share a room when you were a boy?
They didn't use to drive more when they lived in California.
It didn't use to snow more when you were a kid.
Did they use to walk to school every day or take the bus?

Another way to talk about the habitual past, especially when you want to
talk about repeated actions, is to use *would*:

*Every day she would walk into the office with a big smile and say "good
morning!" to all of us.*
*On Saturdays we would wake up early, we'd run downstairs, and we would
eat breakfast while watching Saturday morning cartoons.*
Back then people would use wood or coal to heat their homes.
*Every Christmas my brothers and I would try to stay awake to see Santa
Claus.*

PRACTICE: THE PAST WITH *USED TO* AND *WOULD*
Answer each of the following questions using the cues provided.

1. Would you wake up early to work every morning on the farm? (Yes . . .)
2. Did you use to live in a house or an apartment? (house)
3. Where did you use to go to school when you were a kid? (Kennedy
   Elementary School)
4. Did he use to see his friends every weekend? (No . . .)
5. Where did you use to go on vacation as children? (to the beach)
6. What would your professor wear to class every day? (the same hat)
7. Did you use to live in a small town or a city before you came here? (small
   town)
8. What would they eat for breakfast every day? (cereal)
9. When did she use to wake up before she got a job? (10:00)
10. When did they use to go for a walk together? (every morning)

IF AND *WOULD* IN THE PAST
In Lesson 7 we reviewed the conditional with *if* and *would*. Now let's take
a closer look at how to express an unreal or hypothetical condition in the
past tense. Here are some examples:

If it had rained, we would have stayed inside.
*If Paul hadn't come to the party that night, he never would have met
Kerry.*
*If I had lived on a farm as a child, I would have learned a lot more about
animals.*

As you can see, you use the verb *had* (or *hadn't*) and a past participle after *if*:

*If I **had slept** more . . .*
*If you **had told** the truth . . .*
*If they **hadn't talked** during the movie . . .*

. . . and after *would* you use *have* (or *not have*) plus a past participle.

*. . . I **would have been** more energetic.*
*. . . he **would not have called** you a liar!*
*. . . we **would have enjoyed** ourselves.*

PRACTICE: *IF* AND *WOULD* IN THE PAST
Rewrite each of the following sentences in the past tense. Use the right forms of the verbs provided, and don't forget to use *had* and *would have*!

1. If we (go) to the beach, we (get) a tan.
2. If you (leave) earlier, you (make) your flight.
3. If Harry (study) harder, he (get) a better grade.
4. If Gerard (come) with us, he (have) a good time.
5. If they (go) to bed earlier, they (wake) up in a better mood.
6. If you (take) the subway to work, you (not enjoy) the spring morning.
7. If it (snow) more, they (cancel) school.
8. If Sarah (choose) a different route, she (not miss) the traffic.
9. If we (eat) a little bit earlier, we (leave) the house already.
10. If Wally (finish) his work yesterday, he (stay) home today.

16D LISTENING EXERCISE

🎧 Listen to the recordings and rephrase each of the sentences you hear using the right form of or expression with the word *use*.

1. *She'll adapt to her new job soon.*
2. *He's accustomed to cold winters.*
3. *When I was younger I always went skiing.*
4. *Are you working on the computer right now?*
5. *Are you adjusting to life in the United States?*

ANSWER KEY—PRACTICE SECTIONS

VOCABULARY

1. acquaintance	6. wine	11. mutual friend	16. to adjust
2. hors d'oeuvre	7. small talk	12. interested in	17. recipe
3. get to know	8. adjustment	13. cozy	18. stranger
4. enjoy	9. hobby	14. chatted	19. adapt
5. fan	10. graduation	15. pastimes	20. coincidence

USES OF USE

1. used	4. isn't	6. using	3. used to
2. are	5. gotten	7. get used to	8. used to
3. used to			9. is used to
			10. get

THE PAST WITH USED TO AND WOULD

1. Yes, I would wake up early to work every morning on the farm.
2. I used to live in a house.
3. I used to go to Kennedy Elementary School when I was a kid.
4. No, he didn't use to see his friends every weekend.
5. We used to go to the beach on vacation as children.
6. My professor used to wear the same hat to class every day.
7. I used to live in a small town before I came here.
8. They would eat cereal for breakfast every day.
9. She used to wake up at 10:00 before she got a job.
10. They used to go for a walk together every morning.

IF AND WOULD IN THE PAST

1. If we had gone to the beach, we would have gotten a tan.
2. If you had left earlier, you would have made your flight.
3. If Harry had studied harder, he would have gotten a better grade.
4. If Gerard had come with us, he would have had a good time.
5. If they had gone to bed earlier, they would have woken up in a better mood.
6. If you had taken the subway to work, you would not have enjoyed the spring morning.
7. If it had snowed more, they would have cancelled school.
8. If Sarah had chosen a different route, she wouldn't have missed the traffic.
9. If we had eaten a little bit earlier, we would have left the house already.
10. If Wally had finished his work yesterday, he would have stayed home today.

LISTENING EXERCISE

1. She'll get used to her new job soon.
2. He's used to cold winters.
3. When I was younger I used to go skiing.
4. Are you using the computer right now?
5. Are you getting used to life in the United States?

WEEKEND ACTIVITIES

Lesson 17 will take you to the beach, to a golf course, and to a theater. You'll hear a lot of vocabulary that's handy for talking about what you do when you don't have to work— how you spend your leisure time, in other words. Then you'll take a closer look at some idiomatic uses of the word *what*, as well as noun clauses that begin with the word *what*. Next you'll review noun clauses that begin with other question words, and finally you'll take a look at verbs that can be followed by either gerunds or infinitives, such as *it started raining* or *it started to rain*.

17A DIALOGUE

DIALOGUE 1: WHAT A GREAT DAY!

Let's listen in as June and Randy plan a trip to the beach to take advantage of some great weather. Well, at least June plans the trip—Randy has something else on his mind.

June: *What a great day! Hey, Randy, do you want to go to the beach this weekend?*

Randy: *Yeah, that's a great idea. Maybe Susan and Richard would like to come along.*

June: *I doubt it. They're not seeing each other anymore.*

Randy: *You're kidding!*

June: *No, they split up last week. We should pack beach towels and sunscreen.*

Randy: *What happened?*

June: *I don't really know. Maybe we could have a picnic. What do you think?*

Randy: *I can't believe Susan and Richard. I always thought they'd get married one of these days. What a shame!*

June: *Get over it. It's not like they were a match made in heaven. Let's take sodas and sandwiches.*

Randy: *Sodas and sandwiches? What are you talking about?*

June: *About our picnic at the beach. Have you been listening to me?*

Now listen to the dialogue again. This time, repeat after the native speakers in the pauses provided.

DIALOGUE 2: ARE YOU READY TO PLAY GOLF?

Bob and Jim are getting ready to play some golf. Let's listen to their friendly wager.

Bob: *So glad you could make it to the club today. Are you ready to play golf?*

Jim: *If I were any more ready, you wouldn't stand a chance.*

Bob: *Is that so? What do you say, loser pays for lunch at the club?*

Jim: *Sounds good. I'm looking forward to the exercise.*

Bob: *Do you have all your clubs?*

Jim: *Yup. Wow, what an amazing course!*

Listen to the dialogue a second time, and repeat in the pauses provided.

DIALOGUE 3: I'M SO GLAD YOU GOT TICKETS!

Mary and Ricardo have come to the symphony to hear a very famous orchestra. Read through their conversation as they wait.

Ricardo: *What a beautiful theater!*

Mary: *Yes, it's one of the oldest in the city.*

Ricardo: *Really? I didn't know that.*

Mary: *And the orchestra is world renowned.*

Ricardo: *I didn't know that either. I'm so glad you got tickets!*

Mary: *And I suppose you also didn't know that the conductor just returned from a world tour?*

Ricardo: *Ah, well. Now that you mention it . . . .*

17B WORDS IN ACTION

leisure
When you're not working, you have leisure time.

take advantage of
The weather is beautiful! We should take advantage of it and do something outside.

sunscreen
You should wear sunscreen to protect your skin.

split (or break) up
They were boyfriend and girlfriend, but they split (broke) up last week.

date
I don't go out on many dates.
Richard and Jennifer have been dating each other since they were fifteen.

match
Cindy and Rob are a good match; they're happy together and have a good relationship.

seeing each other
After seeing each other for two years, Roger and Kathy are getting married.

go for a drive/take a drive (the subject is controlling the car)
If you want to conserve gas, you shouldn't go for a drive just for pleasure.
Let's get in the car and take a drive in the country.

go for a ride/take a ride (the subject is the passenger)
I'd like to go for a ride in your car sometime.
You shouldn't take a ride with a stranger.

hiking
I love to go hiking in the woods or in the mountains.

curtain
When the curtain rises, the show begins.

orchestra
Barbara loves classical music, so she goes to hear the orchestra often.

concert
Karl's favorite band is giving a concert this weekend.

stadium
It was an important soccer game, so the stadium was full.

play
I love to go to the theater and see plays.

world renowned
This singer is famous not only in America, she's world renowned.

challenge
Fred challenged Mike to a tennis match.

stand a chance
Mike is a much better player, so Fred doesn't stand a chance against him.

wager
How about a little wager? The loser has to buy the winner a drink.

exercise
It's important to exercise—swimming, running, and weightlifting all keep you healthy.

golf club
The golf club has a very good restaurant where we go before or after a round of golf.
I hope that my new set of golf clubs will improve my game.

work out
Sean goes to the gym and works out every evening.

in shape
Greg stays in shape by going to the gym and swimming every weekend.

course ·
There are eighteen holes on this golf course.

volunteer
Miriam volunteers at a homeless shelter on Sunday mornings.
Mark is a volunteer for an AIDS information hotline.

work around the house
My father likes to work around the house on weekends; he repairs things, cleans,
paints, and works in the yard.

Now turn on the recordings and listen to the vocabulary in bold. Repeat each word or expression, and the example sentence, in the pauses provided.

PRACTICE: VOCABULARY

leisure	orchestra	exercise
took advantage of	concerts	golf clubs
sunscreen	stadium	work out
break up	play	in shape
date	world renowned	course
match	challenge	volunteers
seeing each other	stand a chance	work around the
hiking	wager	house
curtain		

1. Their house is right next to a golf _____.
2. If you think you're a better basketball player than he is, then _____ him to a game!
3. How long have Marsha and David been _____ _____ _____? They act as though they're married.
4. It's important to use _____ at the beach if you don't want to get a bad burn.
5. The _____ was full for the big football game this weekend.
6. The pianist is _____ _____; that's why the tickets were so hard to get.
7. How do you like to spend your _____ time?
8. My father loves to golf, so I got him a new set of _____ _____ for his birthday.
9. Mitchell has a _____ with Gloria tonight; he's been getting ready for hours!
10. If you're so confident that you'll win, then how about a _____ of a few dollars?
11. This weekend I'm going to _____ _____ _____ _____; I have to paint the bedroom and replace the cabinet doors in the kitchen.
12. Shhh! The _____ is about to rise and the show will begin.
13. Jessica _____ at a free clinic on Wednesday nights.
14. Trisha plays the cello in an _____.
15. Pete _____ _____ _____ his day off work and got a lot of errands done.
16. There's a beautiful trail through the forest that's perfect for _____.
17. After all of that food this weekend, I really need to _____!

18. Leroy isn't _____ _____ at all! He climbed two flights of stairs and is completely out of breath.

19. Matt is such a fast runner that you don't _____ _____ _____ in a race against him.

20. When did they _____ _____? They seemed so happy together just two weeks ago!

21. Justin is rehearsing for his role in a _____.

22. Sometimes Derek goes to the gym to _____ _____ on his lunch break.

23. Everyone thinks that Sandy and Pat are a great _____ for each other.

24. I love to go to _____ and hear my favorite bands.

17C TAKE A CLOSER LOOK

USES OF *WHAT*

The word *what* can be used idiomatically, to show shock, surprise, disappointment, anger, or just about any other strong emotion. Listen to the recorded examples.

🎧 *You're from Vermont as well? What a coincidence!*
What a beautiful house!
They split up? What a shame!
It still doesn't work? What a nuisance!
The car won't start? What a drag!

📖 *What* can also be used to introduce entire thoughts that can be the subject or object of a sentence. Take a look at these examples:

What I saw surprised me.
I didn't hear what the speaker said.
I don't know what the capital of North Dakota is.

Technically, the words in bold above are called "noun clauses." A noun clause is a complete thought, with a subject and a verb. It works in the same way any noun can work in a sentence. Take a look at these three sentences, which are the same as the three examples above, except that they use nouns instead of noun clauses.

The film surprised me.
I didn't hear the speech.
I don't know the answer.

Notice that word order in noun clauses introduced by *what* is not the same as word order in questions introduced by *what*. Even though *what* normally begins questions, you should not use question word order. In noun clauses, the subject always has to stay before the verb. And even though the verbs *do, does,* and *did* are used in questions with *what* (*What do you see? What **did** she say? What **does** he write?*) you should not use them in noun clauses (*. . . what you see, . . . what she said, . . . what he writes*). Compare the following pairs of sentences:

What do you see?
*I don't know **what you see**.*

What did she say?
***What she said** is very interesting.*

What does he write?
*He told me **what he writes**.*

What does that word mean?
*The tour guide explained to me **what that word means**.*

What is this man's name?
*I asked my friend **what this man's name is**.*

What are you doing?
*I don't understand **what you are doing**.*

What is he saying?
*I can't hear **what he's saying**.*

What will you do?
*Have you thought about **what you'll do**?*

PRACTICE: USES OF *WHAT*
Write new sentences combining the questions and cues provided. Rephrase the question as a noun phrase. For example, if you see: *What is she saying? I don't understand . . .*, your answer would be: *I don't understand what she is saying.*

1. What will you do? They don't know . . .
2. What does Mrs. Gutierrez eat for breakfast? I have no idea . . .
3. What did she cook for dinner? I didn't like . . .
4. What are they fighting about? Do you know . . . ?
5. What are you writing? Can I read . . . ?
6. What do the kids want? Grandma knows . . .
7. What is he saying? . . . scares me.
8. What do they believe? . . . is their own business.
9. What is the price of that dress? I wonder . . .
10. What are you watching on television? . . . bores me.

NOUN CLAUSES WITH QUESTION WORDS
You've just seen how to use noun clauses with the question word *what*. As you probably know, you can also use other question words to introduce noun clauses. Since you already know so much about noun clauses with

what, there's little more that you have to understand when it comes to noun clauses with *who, where, why, when, how, how much,* and *how many.*

Who is that man?
I don't know **who that man is**.

Who lives here?
The realtor told me **who lives here**.

Where are they going?
Where they are going is dangerous.

Why did you say that?
I'll never understand **why you said that**.

When will you be back tonight?
Tell me **when you'll be back tonight**.

How does he look?
How he looks doesn't concern me.

How much did that car cost?
May I ask you **how much that car cost**?

How many people did you invite to your party?
I can't believe **how many people you invited to your party**!

PRACTICE: NOUN CLAUSES WITH QUESTION WORDS
Once again, write new sentences combining the questions and cues provided, and rephrase the question as a noun phrase.

1. Who was knocking at the door? Betty didn't know . . .
2. When does class start? I asked the professor . . .
3. When will she be home? Barbara doesn't know . . .
4. Where does your friend live? . . . is not very far from here.
5. Why did he get to work late today? Jim's boss wants to know . . .
6. How does the VCR work? Brian still doesn't understand . . .
7. How much do they pay in rent? . . . is none of their neighbor's business!
8. Who gave you that ring? I'm asking . . .
9. How many times has Julia been here? Ryan wanted to know . . .
10. Where do you work? Tell me . . .

VERBS FOLLOWED BY GERUNDS OR INFINITIVES
In Lesson 11 you took a closer look at verbs that are followed by gerunds, such as *to avoid doing something*. In Lesson 12 you saw verbs that are followed by the infinitive, such as *to intend to do something*. Now let's take a look at verbs that can be followed either by the gerund or the infinitive:

It began to rain earlier in the day.
It began raining earlier in the day.

I can't bear to listen to this awful music!
I can't bear listening to this awful music!

She can't stand to walk in the rain.
She can't stand walking in the rain.

They continued to argue late into the night.
They continued arguing late into the night.

We hate to wake up early on Saturdays.
We hate waking up early on Saturdays.

I like to study at night.
I like studying at night.

Mrs. Spencer loves to walk in her garden.
Mrs. Spencer loves walking in her garden.

I would prefer to take the bus.
I would prefer taking the bus.

They started to work at 8:30 today.
They started working at 8:30 today.

Note that there are a few verbs that can be used with a gerund or an infinitive, but they have slightly different meanings:

I forgot calling my friend last night. (I forgot that I called my friend last night.)
I forgot to call my friend last night. (I meant to call my friend, but I forgot.)
Lou remembered going to the store. (He remembered that he went to the store.)
Lou remembered to go to the store. (Lou had to go to the store, and he did it.)

PRACTICE: VERBS FOLLOWED BY GERUNDS OR INFINITIVES
Use the words and phrases below to make complete sentences. There are two correct answers for each one.

1. Mrs. MacMahon prefers // walk // home from work.
2. They say it will start // snow // in the middle of the night.
3. The children can't bear // not know // where their gifts are hidden.
4. The professor continued // speak // after the class was finished.
5. What do you love // do // in your free time?
6. My dog hates // be // away from me.
7. We like // go // running together every morning.
8. I didn't remember // leave // my keys on the table.

17D LISTENING EXERCISE

🎧 Listen to the recorded sentences and comment on them using *what*. Use the cues provided.

1. *This theater is very beautiful.*
2. *I can't believe you live just next door!* (coincidence)
3. *Andrea feels sick today.* (shame)
4. *My watch broke.* (nuisance)

ANSWER KEY—PRACTICE SECTIONS

VOCABULARY

1. course	7. leisure	13. volunteers	19. stand a chance
2. challenge	8. golf clubs	14. orchestra	20. break up
3. seeing each other	9. date	15. took advantage of	21. play
4. sunscreen	10. wager	16. hiking	22. work out
5. stadium	11. work around the house	17. exercise	23. match
6. world renowned	12. curtain	18. in shape	24. concerts

USES OF WHAT

1. They don't know what you will do.
2. I have no idea what Mrs. Gutierrez eats for breakfast.
3. I didn't like what she cooked for dinner.
4. Do you know what they are fighting about?
5. Can I read what you are writing?
6. Grandma knows what the kids want.
7. What he is saying scares me.
8. What they believe is their own business.
9. I wonder what the price of that dress is.
10. What you are watching on television bores me.

NOUN CLAUSES WITH QUESTION WORDS

1. Betty didn't know who was knocking at the door.
2. I asked the professor when the class starts.
3. Barbara doesn't know when she will be home.
4. Where your friend lives is not very far from here.
5. Jim's boss wants to know why he got to work late today.
6. Brian still doesn't understand how the VCR works.
7. How much they pay in rent is none of their neighbor's business!
8. I'm asking who gave you that ring.
9. Ryan wanted to know how many times Julia has been here.
10. Tell me where you work.

VERBS FOLLOWED BY GERUNDS OR INFINITIVES

1. Mrs. MacMahon prefers walking home from work. Mrs. MacMahon prefers to walk home from work.
2. They say it will start snowing in the middle of the night. They say it will start to snow in the middle of the night.
3. The children can't bear not knowing where their gifts are hidden. The children can't bear not to know where their gifts are hidden.
4. The professor continued speaking after the class was finished. The professor continued to speak after the class was finished.
5. What do you love doing in your free time? What do you love to do in your free time?
6. My dog hates being away from me. My dog hates to be away from me.
7. We like going running together every morning. We like to go running together every morning.
8. I didn't remember leaving my keys on the table. I didn't remember to leave my keys on the table.

LISTENING EXERCISE

1. What a beautiful theater!
2. What a coincidence!
3. What a shame!
4. What a nuisance!

Lesson 18

HOLIDAYS

Lesson 18 focuses on holidays. You'll hear two friends discuss their families' Thanksgiving celebrations. You'll also review vocabulary that deals with holidays and celebrations of all kinds. Next you'll review how to use the words *too, also, so, either,* and *neither.* Then you'll take a closer look at verbs that are followed by certain prepositions (*to prepare **for**, to count **on***, etc.) as well as noun clauses that begin with *if* or *whether.*

18A DIALOGUE

LONG TIME, NO SEE!
Doug and Larry are two friends who haven't seen each other in a while.
Let's listen in as they talk about how they spent Thanksgiving.

Doug: *Hi, Larry. Long time, no see.*

Larry: *Doug! What's new?*

Doug: *Nothing much.*

Larry: *How was your Thanksgiving?*

Doug: *Oh, it was great. I slept late.*

Larry: *So did I. We didn't have lunch till three.*

Doug: *I took my little sister to see the Thanksgiving Day parade before dinner. She loved it. Then we had a big family dinner around six.*

Larry: *Who came? Anyone I know?*

Doug: *Well, my older sister and her husband came for the whole weekend. You met her a couple of years ago, remember? And of course, my stepbrother stopped by for dinner on Thursday, and so did my aunts and uncles with all their kids. The oldest is only nine. I had to play games all day long.*

Larry: *What a drag! So, how's your sister doing? I haven't seen her in ages.*

Doug: *She's fine. She loves her new job.*

Larry: *I didn't know she had a new job.*

Doug: *Neither did I. Also, she and Mike just bought a new house.*

Larry: *I see they're really getting into married life. Anyway, we had a small Thanksgiving. Just my parents, my sister, and I. My mom made a great dinner.*

Doug: *Oh, yeah—what did you have?*

Larry: *Well, turkey, of course, but she made this great stuffing with sausages and apples.*

Doug: *Mmm.*

Larry: *Yeah, I really pigged out.*

Doug: *Join the club! My stepmother isn't the best cook. But the turkey was good. I had enough to last me a lifetime. So, did you watch the game?*

Larry: *Are you kidding? Of course. And on a big-screen TV. We just bought it last week.*

Doug: *Wow—next Thanksgiving I'm coming to your house.*

Larry: *Hey, you're missing the point. You're supposed to be with family on Thanksgiving.*

Doug: *I will be—with your family!*

Now listen to the dialogue again, repeating after the native speakers in the pauses provided.

18B WORDS IN ACTION

📖 *day off*
I don't have to work tomorrow; I have a day off.

take off
Are you taking off work tomorrow, or are you coming to the office?

sleep in
I always sleep in on holidays; I like not having to wake up for work.

drag
—Was the parade fun? —No! It was a real drag!

parade
My little brother likes to watch all the people marching by in the parade.

to get into
I've been reading this book for a week, but I can't get into it! It still doesn't interest me.
—Does Jack like his new job? —Yeah, he's really getting into it!

to observe
Are you coming to work tomorrow, or will you be observing the religious holiday?

observances
The post office and banks are all closed tomorrow for religious observances.

personal day
I'm taking a personal day next week. My family is in town and I'd like to spend the day with them.

reception
After the wedding ceremony, we all went to the reception for dinner, drinks, and dancing.

stepbrothers
My mother's new husband has two sons, which means I have two new stepbrothers.

join the club!
—I really need to exercise and get in shape. —Join the club! I feel the same way!

to miss the point
You don't understand what I'm saying at all. You're really missing the point.

to throw a party
Kenny is out of the hospital, so we're throwing him a party to welcome him home.

anniversary
My parents have been married for thirty years, and we're throwing them an anniversary party.

stuffing
We always fill the turkey with sausage stuffing.

packed
—Were there a lot of people at your parents' for Thanksgiving? —Yeah, it was packed!

to pig out
I ate too much. I really pigged out.

get together
My family always has a holiday get together; it's nice for everyone to spend some time together.
We need to get together more often; I never see you any more!

to stop by
Why don't you stop by for a beer tonight?

surprise party
It's Cindy's birthday, and we're having a surprise party for her. Don't tell her!

toast
We all toasted one another at midnight on New Year's Eve.

🎧 Now turn on the recordings and listen to the vocabulary in bold. Repeat each word or expression, and the example sentence, in the pauses provided.

PRACTICE: VOCABULARY

day off	personal day	stuffing
take off	reception	packed
sleep in	stepbrothers	pig out
drag	join the club	get together
parade	missing the point	stop by
get into	throw a party	surprise parties
observe	anniversary	toast
observances		

1.   Don't each too much! You'll be sorry if you _____ _____!
2.   The wedding _____ was held in the hall of a beautiful hotel.
3.   Everyone in town lines Main Street to watch the _____ on Veteran's Day.

4.   You're tired after the party, too? _____ _____ _____!
5.   Yasmine doesn't like _____ _____. She always likes to be prepared.
6.   How do you _____ Ramadan?
7.   Don't call me before 11:00 tomorrow. I plan to _____ _____.
8.   Kara needs to relax. She hasn't had a _____ _____ in months.
9.   On Thanksgiving we always put apples and walnuts in the _____.
10. Everyone raise your glasses. I'd like to make a _____.
11. Kurt is going to _____ _____ _____ for his friend's birthday on Friday.
12. Dorothy can't _____ _____ the book she's reading. It doesn't interest her.
13. This party is a real _____! I'm not enjoying myself at all.
14. There are so many people in this room! It's really _____.
15. Terry has some important errands she has to run tomorrow, so she took a _____ _____.
16. Next Tuesday is our fifth _____ so we're going out to dinner.
17. Pavel is having a party next Saturday, and he asked us to _____ _____.
18. No! You're _____ _____ _____. That's not what I mean at all.
19. The office will be closed tomorrow for religious _____.
20. Wendy wants to _____ _____ next week for a trip to Puerto Rico.
21. Henry's mother's second husband has two sons, so Henry has two _____.
22. We're having a small _____ _____ for the Fourth of July. Please come.

18C TAKE A CLOSER LOOK

TOO, ALSO, SO, EITHER, AND NEITHER
Turn on the CD and listen to the recorded examples of how to use these common words.

🎧 *My sister is home. Her husband is home, too.*
My sister is home and so is her husband.
My uncle didn't see the game. I didn't either.
My uncle didn't see the game, and neither did I.
I will watch the game.
So will I.
My brother can't spend Thanksgiving with us.
Neither can mine.

📖 As you can see from the examples, *so* and *too* are used with positive expressions, while *neither* and *either* are used with negative expressions. Notice that *neither*, although used in a negative sentence, does not require a form of *not* with the verb.

The word order is also different depending on which word is being used. Sentences using *so* and *neither* follow the order of **so/neither** + *verb* + *subject*, whereas sentences using *too* and *either* are *subject* + *verb* + **too/either**.

So do I.
Neither do I.
I do too.
I don't either.

Take a look at these examples using *also* and *too*:

John went to the movies. Lamont also went to the movies.
I'd like a glass of milk. I'd like a glass of water, also.
I'm going horseback riding tomorrow. My sister is too.
Put this book back on the shelf. Put this vase on the shelf, too.

PRACTICE: *TOO*, *ALSO*, *SO*, *EITHER*, AND *NEITHER*
Write new sentences using the cues provided. For example, if you see: I'm going to the party this weekend. (Tim, too) the correct answer is: Tim is going to the party this weekend, too.

1.   Brenda is going to stop by tonight. (Mike, so)
2.   You didn't like the movie. (I, either)
3.   You didn't like the movie. (I, neither)
4.   Norman throws great parties. (Ben, too)
5.   Tom is taking a personal day tomorrow. (Glen, also)
6.   You think this movie is a drag. (I, so)

VERBS FOLLOWED BY PREPOSITIONS
In the dialogue you heard Doug say that his stepbrothers *stopped by* for dinner. As you know, verbs are very often followed by certain prepositions in English. Some verbs can be followed by more than one preposition, and some can have their meaning changed slightly depending on what preposition follows. Let's take a look at many of the most common and useful examples of verbs followed by prepositions:

agree with
*Frank doesn't **agree with** Sarah **about** where to go on vacation.*

apologize to . . . for
*Justin **apologized to** Andrew **for** what he said.*

apply for
*I **applied for** a job in a restaurant yesterday.*

apply to
*Meagan has **applied to** many different colleges already.*

argue with/about
Sandy is **arguing with** Jake **about** something again.

believe in
David doesn't **believe in** God, so he doesn't observe religious holidays.

blame for
Who will they **blame for** this mess?

call about
I **called** the doctor **about** my appointment on Friday.

call for
It's your anniversary? This **calls for** a toast!

care about
Gerard doesn't **care about** his job.

check in with
I called the office to **check in with** my boss.

compare to
You can't **compare** the movie to the book!

count on
You can **count on** me!

cover with
Trish **covered** the table **with** a new tablecloth.

cry about
What is the baby **crying about**?

decide on
Have you **decided on** a restaurant?

depend on
Bob can't **depend on** Erik to help him.

dream of
They **dream of** taking a trip to China.

excel at
Vincent really **excels at** languages; he should study linguistics.

feel like
I don't **feel like** going out tonight. Can we stay in?

fight against
The government is **fighting against** rebel forces.

fight for
People everywhere are **fighting for** their freedom.

fight with/over
Paul is **fighting with** his brother Tim **over** the car.

fill with
He **filled** the vase **with** water.

forget about
It's raining so hard! We can **forget about** going to the beach.

forgive for
Forgive me **for** being so mean to you.

go for
I could really **go for** Thai food tonight.

go to jail for
You could **go to jail for** tax fraud.

hide from
The cat is **hiding from** us; she's behind the couch.

hope for
The best we can do is **hope for** peace.

insist upon
Laurie **insists upon** coming with us.

interest in
My friend Nick **interested** me **in** soccer.

look at
Look at the sky! It's an odd color.

look forward to
We really **look forward to** meeting you.

look out for
If you go skating, **look out for** thin ice.

participate in
Do you want to **participate in** the meeting tomorrow?

pray for
People of many different religions got together to **pray for** peace.

prepare for
We **prepared for** the storm by closing the windows and getting everything inside.

prevent from
They tried to **prevent** the protestors **from** crossing the street.

protect from
Keith's big brother **protects** him **from** bullies.

provide with
They **provided** us **with** food and clothing after the fire.

qualify for
You don't **qualify for** a loan from this bank.

recover from
Shawn has **recovered from** his surgery.

rely on
You can't **rely on** the trains to be on time.

respond to
Joseph still hasn't **responded to** the e-mail he received.

save for
I've been **saving for** a new car since last June.

stand up for
Don't be scared! **Stand up for** your rights.

stare at
Don't **stare at** that lady! It's rude.

stop by
We **stopped by** the party but didn't stay very long.

stop from
We've tried everything to **stop** the cat **from** scratching the sofa!

strive for
The company says that it **strives for** excellence.

tease about
Her classmates **tease** Sally **about** her glasses.

thank for
He **thanked** me **for** my help.

think about
What are you **thinking about**?

vote for
Which candidate did you **vote for**?

work toward
We have to **work toward** a solution to this problem.

worry about
Don't **worry about** me; I'll be fine.

PRACTICE: VERBS FOLLOWED BY PREPOSITIONS
Complete each of the following sentences with the correct preposition.

1. I don't agree _____ what you're saying.
2. You should apologize _____ him _____ that!
3. Don't count _____ him to help you!
4. Could you fill the pot _____ hot water?
5. You should use sunscreen to protect yourself _____ sunburn.
6. What on earth are you staring _____?
7. They haven't decided _____ a marketing plan yet.
8. We insist _____ doing this the right way.
9. It's hot. I could go _____ drink.
10. Let's hope _____ the best outcome possible.
11. Don't blame me _____ your problems!
12. The criminal hid _____ the police in an abandoned building.
13. I really don't feel _____ cooking tonight. Let's go out.
14. Ricky doesn't participate _____ classroom activities.
15. She's worried _____ her husband; he's traveling in this awful weather.
16. Thank you so much _____ all your help!
17. What are they arguing _____ again?
18. I don't care _____ what they think.
19. Look out _____ that woman crossing the street! Drive more carefully.
20. The rebels say that they're fighting _____ their rights.
21. Have you all prepared _____ the test tomorrow?
22. Amrita doesn't believe _____ eating animals; it's against her religion.
23. Bill started saving _____ a house when he was only 18.
24. Have you responded _____ the invitation to Judy's wedding yet?
25. The guard prevented us _____ getting into the building without ID.

NOUN CLAUSES WITH *IF* AND *WHETHER*
In Lesson 17 you reviewed how to change a question beginning with a question word into a noun phrase, which is part of a longer sentence:

What is his name?
I don't know what his name is.

Now let's take a look at how to change a yes/no question into a noun phrase that you can use as part of a longer sentence. Simply add either *if* or *whether*, and follow the same rules about word order and use of *did*, *do*, and *does*:

Is his name John?
I don't know if his name is John.
I don't know whether his name is John.

Does he work here?
I can't tell you if he works here.
I can't tell you whether he works here.

Did they come to the party last night?
Can you tell me if they came to the party last night?
Can you tell me whether they came to the party last night?

Note that both *if* and *whether* are correct in all of these cases, but *if* is more conversational.

PRACTICE: NOUN CLAUSES WITH *IF* AND *WHETHER*
Combine the following sentences and phrases together to form one longer sentence with a noun phrase. Use either *if* or *whether*; both are correct.

1. Is Sandra taking a day off tomorrow? (I'm not sure . . .)
2. Did they have a good time last night? (No one knows . . .)
3. Will everyone be in tomorrow? (. . . is not important.)
4. Do you take Fridays off from work? (Could you tell me . . .)
5. Does this company have a dress code? (I'd like to know . . .)
6. Have they decided on a place to meet? (They're telling us . . .)
7. Are you throwing a surprise party for me? (I would like to know . . .)
8. Would you buy that shirt if you had the money? (We're asking . . .)

18D LISTENING EXERCISE

🎧 Listen to the recorded sentences and form new sentences using the cues provided along with the words *so* or *neither.*

1. *I had turkey this Thanksgiving.* (I)
2. *The Bergers watched the game on T.V.* (Simpsons)
3. *Peter shouldn't drink so much.* (Mary)
4. *I can't eat any more.* (I)
5. *I won't be able to see the parade.* (you)

ANSWER KEY—PRACTICE SECTIONS

VOCABULARY

1. pig out	7. sleep in	13. drag	19. observances
2. reception	8. day off	14. packed	20. take off
3. parade	9. stuffing	15. personal day	21. stepbrothers
4. Join the club	10. toast	16. anniversary	22. get together
5. surprise parties	11. throw a party	17. stop by	
6. observe	12. get into	18. missing the point	

TOO, ALSO, SO, EITHER AND NEITHER

1. So is Mike.
2. I didn't either. (I didn't like the movie either.)
3. Neither did I.
4. Ben does, too. (Ben throws great parties, too.)
5. Glen is taking a personal day tomorrow also. (Glen is also taking a personal day tomorrow.)
6. So do I.

VERBS FOLLOWED BY PREPOSITIONS

1. with	8. upon	15. about	22. in
2. to, for	9. for	16. for	23. for
3. on	10. for	17. about	24. to
4. with	11. for	18. about	25. from
5. from	12. from	19. for	
6. at	13. like	20. for	
7. on	14. in	21. for	

NOUN CLAUSES WITH IF AND WHETHER

1. I'm not sure whether/if Sandra is taking a day off tomorrow.
2. No one knows whether/if they had a good time last night.
3. Whether/if everyone will be in tomorrow is not important.
4. Could you tell me whether/if you take Fridays off from work?
5. I'd like to know whether/if this company has a dress code.
6. They're telling us whether/if they've decided on a place to meet.
7. I would like to know whether/if you're throwing a surprise party for me.
8. We're asking whether/if you would buy that shirt if you had the money.

LISTENING EXERCISE

1. So did I.
2. So did the Simpsons.
3. Neither should Mary.
4. Neither can I.
5. Neither will you.

Lesson 19
MONEY

In Lesson 19 you'll go to the bank, so naturally you'll review a lot of important vocabulary that deals with money, banking, and personal finance. Then you'll review several different ways to express desire with *want*, *would like*, *wish*, and *if only*. Finally, you'll take a closer look at verbs that are followed by objects and infinitives, such as *to allow someone to do something*.

19A DIALOGUE

I'D LIKE TO DEPOSIT A CHECK

Andrew Keller has a few things he needs to take care of at the bank. Let's listen in.

Andrew: *Hi. I'd like to deposit this check into my savings account.*

Teller: *OK. That gives you a new balance of $956.*

Andrew: *Thanks. Can I order new checks with you as well?*

Teller: *No, customer service will take care of that.*
(AT THE CUSTOMER SERVICE COUNTER)

Andrew: *Hi. I'd like to order new checks.*

Customer
Service: *What's your account number?*

Andrew: *I wish I could find my checkbook! I must have left it at home. I'm sorry, but I don't know the number by heart.*

Customer
Service: *That's okay. If you give me your name, I'll check my computer.*

Andrew: *Andrew Keller.*

Customer
Service: *And your social security number?*

Andrew: *233-56-7390.*

Customer
Service: *Okay, here you are. Would you like a box of five hundred or one thousand checks?*

Andrew: *Five hundred will do for now.*

Customer
Service: *Would you like your address printed on your checks?*

Andrew: *Yes, and my phone number, please.*

Customer
Service: *No problem. I'll put the order in today. They'll be mailed directly to you.*

Andrew: *Thanks. Also, I'm interested in getting a car loan. Do you happen to know what the interest rates are?*

Customer
Service: *That depends on the amount you borrow. But you'll have to talk to one of our loan officers.*

Andrew: *I see. Where can I find a loan officer?*

Customer
Service: *Our loan department is located on the second floor.*

Andrew: *Thanks. One last question. Do you have any credit card applications?*

Customer
Service: *Yes, here's one.*

Andrew: *Can I use your ATM machines with this card?*

Customer
Service: *Absolutely.*
Andrew: *You've been very helpful. Thank you.*
Customer
Service: *You're welcome.*

Now listen to the dialogue again. This time, repeat after the native speakers in the pauses provided.

19B WORDS IN ACTION

 account
I have a checking account and a savings account at that bank.

open
Brendan needs to open an account at a local bank because he just moved here.

close
—Do you still have an account here? —No, I closed it.

deposit
Would you like to deposit this check into your checking account?

direct deposit
Lenny's company has direct deposit at his bank, so he doesn't have to deposit his paychecks.

withdraw
No, I don't want to deposit the money; I want to withdraw it.

withdrawal
I made a withdrawal from my savings account yesterday.

customer service
Customer service deals with the problems and questions of customers.

teller
Mrs. Klein works as a teller at the bank. She helps people who come in to do their banking.

ATM
If you use an ATM you can make deposits or withdrawals at any time.

PIN
You need to use a personal identification number, or PIN, to use your ATM card.

loan
If you don't have enough money to buy a car, you might be able to get a loan.

mortgage
A mortgage is a loan for a house.

interest rate
Every credit card has a different interest rate.

interest
Savings accounts earn interest.

money market
A money market account earns a little more interest than a savings account.

invest
Robert invests in the stock market.

charge
Would you like to pay cash, or charge it to your credit card?

debit card
You can pay with your debit card, which takes money right out of your bank account.

check
Always remember to carry a photo ID when you write a check.

cash
You can pay by cash, check, or credit card. I need to cash this check for $150.

endorse
When you write a check, you need to sign, or endorse, it.

balance a checkbook
Susan always balances her checkbook; she keeps track of exactly how much money is in her checking account.

statement
Every month the bank sends its customers statements that list all deposits and withdrawals.

🎧 Now turn on the recordings and listen to the vocabulary in bold. Repeat each word or expression, and the example sentence, in the pauses provided.

PRACTICE: VOCABULARY

account	teller	invests
open	ATM	charge
close	PIN	debit card
deposits	loan	check
direct deposit	mortgage	cashed
withdrew	interest rate	endorse
withdrawal	interest	balance a checkbook
customer service	money markets	statement

1. Since my company uses _____ _____ for my paychecks, I almost never go to the bank.
2. What's the _____ _____ on this credit card?
3. I don't have any cash, but can I write a _____?
4. Ben still hasn't _____ the check he got two weeks ago.
5. Walt wrote a check for the merchandise, but he forgot to _____ it.
6. Do you have an _____ at this bank, sir?
7. No, but I'd like to _____ one. I just moved here.
8. I'm paying off my car _____ each month.
9. I needed some cash late last night, but I couldn't find an _____ anywhere.
10. Gordon _____ some money from his savings account to pay for the trip.
11. Every month she _____ $200 into her savings account.
12. Put your money in a savings account so it earns some _____.
13. _____ _____ earn more interest than regular savings accounts.
14. I don't want to make a deposit, but a _____ instead.
15. Complaints and questions are handled by the _____ _____ department.
16. I waited in line until the _____ told me to come to the window.
17. We make monthly _____ payments to pay for the house.
18. I always joke that I can't _____ _____ _____; I never know how much money is in my checking account.
19. I don't have enough cash on me, so I want to _____ it to my credit card.
20. Tony is moving away and needs to _____ all of his accounts.
21. I got my bank _____ in the mail yesterday.
22. Daniel only _____ in stocks from companies that he trusts.
23. I can't use my ATM card; I forgot my _____!
24. You can pay in this store with cash, by check, credit, or _____ _____.

19C TAKE A CLOSER LOOK

EXPRESSING DESIRE
Turn on your CD and listen to several of the different ways you can express desire in English.

I want to deposit this check.
I'd like to order new checks.
I wish I could find my checkbook, but I can't.
I wish I had enough money to buy a new car, but I don't.
I wish the bank would lower the interest rates.
I wish Roger would write more often.
I wish you would stop complaining.
I wish you would pay your bills on time.
I wish I had more time.
If only I had more time.

As you can see, the most common ways to express desire are with *want, would like, wish,* and *if only.* After *want* and *would like,* you just have to use an infinitive:

*I want **to take** tomorrow off.*
*He would like me **to stay** late at work.*

Let's take a special look at *wish* and *if only,* because you need to use special verb forms after them. These forms change depending on when your wish would take place—in the future, the present, or the past.

If you're wishing for something in the future, use *would, could,* or *were going to.*

*I wish they **would come** visit next weekend.*
*If only they **could take** their vacation next month!*
*They wish we **were going to spend** the holidays with them.*
*They wish we **would spend** the holidays with them.*

If you're wishing for something right now, or in general, use the past form of the verb. For *to be,* always use *were.*

*I wish I **could speak** more languages.*
*Mrs. Smith wishes her kids **came** home from college more often.*
*The boy wishes it **were snowing** right now.*
*If only it **weren't raining** so hard!*

And finally, if you're wishing for something in the past, use the past perfect:

*I wish they **had gotten** here a little bit earlier.*
*We wish you **had been** on time this morning.*
*If only the bank **had offered** better interest rates.*
*If only we **hadn't invested** in that company!*

PRACTICE: EXPRESSING DESIRE
Complete each of the following sentences using the correct forms of the words given in parentheses.

1. Kelly wants _____ a money market account. (open)
2. I would like _____ this check, please. (cash)
3. If only she _____ her mother more often. (call)
4. They wish they _____ stay longer. (can)
5. I don't want _____ by check. (pay)
6. If only you _____ more careful with your money! (be)

7. They wish they _____ a little bit earlier to the party last week. (come)
8. They would like _____ told about any changes. (be)
9. My boss wishes we _____ more productive. (be)
10. If only you always _____ me the truth! (tell)
11. We wish it _____ not snowing right now. (be)
12. They wish they _____ in a more interesting city. (live)

VERBS FOLLOWED BY AN OBJECT AND AN INFINITIVE

Take a look at the following sentences:

I want to cook dinner.
I want you to cook dinner.

You've already seen a lot of verbs that are followed by infinitives. *Want* is one of them, but *want* can also be followed by both an object and an infinitive, as in the second example above. Let's take a look at some other important examples.

*My stock broker **advised me to sell** my stocks.*
*Mrs. Peterson wouldn't **allow her children to stay** out so late!*
*We **asked them not to play** their music so loud.*
*I **beg you to tell** me the secret!*
*They **bring their kids to see** the ships in the harbor.*
*I **challenged him to play** chess with me.*
*Sandra **chose me to work** on the proposal with her.*
*The guards **commanded the prisoners to stop**.*
*I **dare you to eat** that entire cake.*
*The teller **directed me to go** to the second floor.*
*We **encourage all of you to study** hard while you're here.*
*The professor **expects his students to read** all of their assignments.*
*Mother **forbids us to watch** television after 9:00!*
*They **forced me to tell** them the truth.*
*We **hired a new assistant to help** with the account.*
*We **invited them to stay** at the cabin for a few days.*
*The captain **ordered the soldiers not to shoot**.*
*We can't **persuade them to stop** spending so much money.*
*He **prepared the students to pass** their final exams.*
*Could you **remind me to take** these documents to the bank?*
*We **require our customers to have** a minimum balance in their accounts.*
*Did they **send you to convince** me to come to the party?*
*Mrs. Nakamura **taught me to speak** Japanese.*
*She **told me not to touch** the computer.*
*We **urge you to take** your time and work carefully.*
*My friend **warned me not to see** that film.*

PRACTICE: VERBS FOLLOWED BY AN OBJECT
AND AN INFINITIVE

Answer each of the following questions using the cues provided.

1.   What did she advise you to do? (open an account)
2.   Where did the teller tell Andrew to go? (second floor)
3.   Who challenged him to play tennis? (his girlfriend)
4.   Who taught him to cook so well? (his mother)
5.   Where did they invite you to spend the weekend? (at their beach house)
6.   What did the teacher encourage you to do? (study hard)
7.   What did they dare you to do? (not go to the meeting)
8.   Who persuaded him not to go on the trip? (I)
9.   What did he urge you not to do? (spend too much money)
10. What did they prepare us to do? (meet with the clients)

19D LISTENING EXERCISE

🎧 Listen to the recorded sentences and restate each one starting with
"*I wish...*"

1.   *I don't have a credit card.*
2.   *Please, help me.*
3.   *I don't know my account number by heart.*
4.   *The bank doesn't offer interest-free loans.*
5.   *I can't go on vacation.*

ANSWER KEY—PRACTICE SECTIONS

VOCABULARY

1. direct deposit	8. loan	14. withdrawal	19. charge
2. interest rate	9. ATM	15. customer service	20. close
3. check	10. withdrew	16. teller	21. statement
4. cashed	11. deposits	17. mortgage	22. invests
5. endorse	12. interest	18. balance a checkbook	23. PIN
6. account	13. Money markets		24. debit card
7. open			

EXPRESSING DESIRE

1. to open	4. could	7. had come	10. told
2. to cash	5. to pay	8. to be	11. were
3. called	6. were	9. were	12. lived

VERBS FOLLOWED BY AN OBJECT AND AN INFINITIVE

1. She advised me/us to open an account.
2. The teller told Andrew to go to the second floor.
3. His girlfriend challenged him to play tennis.
4. His mother taught him to cook so well.
5. They invited me/us to spend the weekend at their beach house.
6. The teacher encouraged me/us to study hard.
7. They dared me/us not go to the meeting.
8. I persuaded him not to go on the trip.
9. He urged me/us not to spend too much money.
10. They prepared us to meet with the clients.

LISTENING EXERCISE

1. I wish I had a credit card.
2. I wish you'd help me.
3. I wish I knew my account number by heart.
4. I wish the bank would offer interest-free loans.
5. I wish I could go on vacation.

Lesson 20

JURY DUTY

Lesson 20 focuses on a civic duty that a lot of people do not like very much—jury duty. As you can imagine, you'll hear a lot of vocabulary that deals with the law and going to court. Then you'll take a closer look at idiomatic uses of a very common verb that we also saw in our very first lesson—*to get*. You'll also review noun clauses with infinitives (*what to do...where to go...*) and adjectives that are followed by certain prepositions, such as *finished with*. (As in: After this lesson, you'll be *finished with* this course!)

20A DIALOGUE

HAS THE JURY REACHED A VERDICT?
Rosa was called for jury duty last week, and she was surprised to find it
very interesting. Let's listen in as she tells her friend Daniel about the case.

Daniel: *Where were you last week, Rosa?*
Rosa: *On jury duty.*
Daniel: *Really? I've never been on a jury. I'm curious—what's it
like?*
Rosa: *Actually, it was quite interesting. The alleged criminal
was a young man. He was tried for theft.*
Daniel: *And did he do it?*
Rosa: *Not so fast. He'd been arrested for stealing a TV. But he
claimed to have bought it.*
Daniel: *So what happened?*
Rosa: *The prosecuting attorney asked him a bunch of
questions.*
Daniel: *Like what?*
Rosa: *Where he had bought the TV, how much he had paid
for it, and stuff like that.*
Daniel: *Did he have an alibi?*
Rosa: *Well, the defendant claimed he was at home by
himself. But there was a witness who saw him coming
out of the store.*
Daniel: *So, he did it?*
Rosa: *Well, we found him guilty.*
Daniel: *Is he in prison now?*
Rosa: *No, the judge released him on bail. He has to come back
for sentencing in a couple of weeks.*
Daniel: *How much time do you think he'll get?*
Rosa: *I don't think he'll serve time. He'll probably get away
with community service.*
Daniel: *It's sad to see a young guy get into trouble, isn't it?*

Now listen to the dialogue again. This time, repeat after the native
speakers in the pauses provided.

20B WORDS IN ACTION

duty
It's a duty—it's our responsibility to do it.

curious
Children are curious about a lot of things and ask many questions.

to steal
Someone stole my wallet! My wallet has been stolen!

thief
A person who steals is a thief.

theft
Theft is a crime—it's illegal to steal things.

judge
The judge watches over the whole trial.

arrest
The police arrested Mr. Gandon for drunk driving.

claim
Mr. Gandon claimed that he was just tired, but they knew he'd been drinking.

to charge
They charged him with a crime and brought him to the police station.

to prosecute
He was prosecuted for his crime—he was charged and brought before a judge for a legal punishment for his crime.

attorney
You have the right to an attorney.

D.A. (District Attorney)
District attorneys represent "the people"—they prosecute people who are accused of breaking the law.

defense attorney
If you're charged with a crime, you need a defense attorney to represent you.

defendant
The prosecution has to prove that the defendant committed the crime.

alibi
He was charged with robbery, but he had an alibi—he was at a restaurant when the crime was committed.

allegedly
The defendant allegedly stole some money.

suspect
John is a suspect in a criminal investigation; the detectives think he may have committed a crime.

bail
The defendant was able to pay bail, so he doesn't have to go to prison before his trial begins.

witness
The witness saw the crime happen.
I witnessed a terrible car accident this morning.

jury
The jury finds the defendant either guilty or not guilty.

trial
During the trial both the prosecution and the defense try to convince the jury of their arguments.

a bunch of
He didn't ask only one, but a bunch of questions.

to serve (or do) time
Kurt is serving (doing) time in prison for stealing cars.

sentence
I think he'll get a short prison sentence, since this is his first arrest.

🎧 Now turn on the recordings and listen to the vocabulary in bold. Repeat each word or expression, and the example sentence, in the pauses provided.

PRACTICE: VOCABULARY

📖

duty	charged	suspect
curious	prosecutes	bail
stolen	attorney	witnessed
thief	district attorney	jury
theft	defense attorney	trial
judge	defendant	a bunch of .
arrested	alibi	done time
claimed	allegedly	sentence

1. There are twelve members of a _____ who decide whether a person is guilty.
2. Kelly studied law and now she's an _____ with a well known law firm.
3. My car's been _____!
4. He got a _____ of five to eight years in prison for his crimes.
5. I've never visited a prison; I'm _____ about what it's like.
6. The police _____ the woman in her house and took her to the police station.
7. Since the crime hasn't been proven, the newspaper article says that the suspect _____ stole the car.

8. The _____ in the case is a man accused of stealing cars.
9. When her purse was stolen, the woman yelled, "Stop! _____!"
10. You may not want to do this, but you have to—it's your _____.
11. Have you ever _____ a crime and been questioned by the police?
12. Because Frank failed the roadside test, he was brought to court and _____ with driving under the influence.
13. Kevin said he didn't do it. He _____ that he was innocent.
14. The police questioned a _____ in the robbery. They think they know who did it.
15. Stuart works for the office of the _____ _____; he likes representing the public against criminals.
16. You can't steal a car! Auto _____ is a serious crime!
17. The district attorney _____ people for many different kinds of crimes.
18. When Robert was accused of a very serious crime, he decided to find the best _____ _____ he could to represent him.
19. The _____ watches over the whole case and makes sure that the law is followed.
20. The reporter knows the attorney well; he's watched her in court _____ _____ _____ times before.
21. Jordan was accused of the crime, but he had a good _____; he was out of town on vacation when it happened.
22. Do you know anyone who has _____ _____ in prison before?
23. For a _____ you need a judge, a jury, a defendant, a defense attorney, and a prosecuting attorney.
24. Mr. Taylor didn't go to prison before his trial—he's out on _____.

20C TAKE A CLOSER LOOK

USES OF *GET*
As you know, the verb *get* can be used in many different ways. Turn on your recordings to listen to examples of just a few:

It can mean *receive*:

I think I should get a raise.
You'll get the letter tomorrow.

It can mean *become*:

It can get very hot in New Orleans.
If you're not careful, you'll get sick.

It can mean *obtain*:

You can get stamps at the post office.
I'll have to get a copy of that.

It can mean *understand*:

Now I get it.
I just don't get the point of this story.

Get to means *arrive at* or *go to*:

How do I get to Thompson Street?
I didn't have a chance to get to the bank yet.

And don't forget that it's used in causatives and many idiomatic expressions:

I'll get the car fixed tomorrow.
This time you won't get away with that.
Can I get back to you on that matter?
Lucy got into trouble again.
Could someone get the phone, please?

Let's look at some more idiomatic expressions with the verb get:

get
It's raining. Can I get you a cab?

get along
How are you getting along at your new job? Are you happy there?

get along with
Do you get along with your new colleagues? Or do you dislike them?

get away
I want to take a short trip out of the city this weekend. I need to get away!

get away with
The police arrested the thief. He didn't get away with his crime.

get back
Oh, you're back home in New York! When did you get back?

get back at
If you do something bad to me, I'll get back at you and do something bad to you.

get better
How long have you been sick? I hope you get better soon!

get even
Jack got even with me for the joke I played on him—he played one on me, too.

get in
—Have you been home long? —No, I just got in.

get in shape
Charles is going to get in shape; he joined a gym and has started jogging.

get in touch
I've been trying to get in touch with you, but your phone has been busy.

get into
Dennis has really gotten into being a policeman. He loves it!

get lost
We're driving without a map, and we don't know where we are. We'll get lost!

get off
Gary's wife was mad at him, but he got off the hook by apologizing and buying roses.

get off of
I usually get off of work at 5:30, and I go straight home.

get (something) off one's chest
I have something to tell you; I really need to get it off my chest.

get on with
You keep stopping your story! Get on with it! We want to hear how it ends.

get one's way
Samantha has to get her way. If things aren't the way she likes them, she gets angry.

get out of
Jake doesn't want to go on jury duty. He's going to try to get out of it.

get (something) out of
—Do you enjoy your book club? —Not anymore. I'm not getting anything out of it.

get out of line
If the kids get out of line the teacher gives them extra homework as a punishment.

get over
Poor Richard still hasn't gotten over his breakup with Sarah. He's very sad.

get rid of
If you want to come in my house, you have to get rid of that cigarette.

get serious
Okay, stop joking. We need to get serious.

get the better of
Don't be upset about that jerk. Don't let him get the better of you!

get through
Fabrizio thinks college is too much work. He doesn't know how he'll get through it.

get through to
Do you understand yet? Am I finally getting through to you?

get to
—Have you gotten to that report yet? —No, I'll start it in fifteen minutes.

get up
What time do you get up in the morning?

get up the courage
Laura wants to ask Mick out on a date, but she hasn't gotten up the courage yet.

PRACTICE: USES OF *GET*
Complete each of the following sentences with the correct idiomatic expression of get.

1. Okay, we've had enough fun for now. Let's _____ _____.
2. Len has something he needs to tell us and _____ _____ _____ _____.
3. We _____ _____ on a back road. We had no idea where we were!
4. I still can't _____ _____ the fact that Paul and Helen broke up. That's so sad.
5. You need to _____ _____ the courage to do what has to be done.
6. I need to _____ _____ _____ _____ Bonnie. Do you have her phone number?
7. You beat me last time, but I'll win this time and _____ _____ with you!
8. They flew to New Zealand for vacation, but they _____ _____ the other day.
9. When you were a kid did you _____ _____ _____ your sisters?
10. You always have to _____ _____ _____! Why can't we do something I want to do?
11. This project is so much work. I don't know how we'll _____ _____ it.

12. I find the club very interesting and inspiring. I _____ a lot _____ _____ it.
13. We're going to the country for a few days. We need to _____ _____ from the city.
14. Roy's parents tried very hard to _____ _____ _____ him, but he still causes trouble and gets bad grades in school.
15. She stole $200? How does she think she'll _____ _____ _____ it?

NOUN CLAUSES WITH INFINITIVES

In Lessons 17 and 18 we reviewed noun clauses with question words and noun clauses with *if* or *whether*. Now we're going to review one more kind of noun clause, and that's a noun clause with an infinitive. Take a look at the following sentences:

*I don't know **where to go**.*
*Dana asked me **what to do**.*
*I'm thinking about **what to say to her about the project**.*
***The person to speak to** about this is Mrs. Fletcher on the third floor.*

The words in bold are all noun clauses with infinitives in them. Notice that they can all be rephrased using *should* or *must* or *have to* or *want to*, etc.:

*I don't know **where I should go**.*
*Dana asked me **what she must do**.*
*I'm thinking about **what I want to say to her about the project**.*
***The person you need to speak to** is Mrs. Fletcher on the third floor.*

So, whenever you see a noun clause with an infinitive, you know that it's just another way of saying *should, must, have to, need to, want to*, etc.

I don't know what I want to eat.
I don't know what to eat.
Please tell me where to go.
Please tell me where I should go.
You can't tell her what to do!
You can't tell her what she has to do!
The book you need to buy is this one.
The book to buy is this one.

PRACTICE: NOUN CLAUSES WITH INFINITIVES
Rewrite each of the following sentences using noun clauses with infinitives.

1. I don't know what I should write.
2. Sarah asked the guard where she had to go.

3. The kids don't know what they want to eat.
4. Have you decided where we should eat tonight?
5. They keep telling me what I must do.
6. Don't tell her what she should say to him!
7. Professor Mackenzie told us what we needed to read tonight.
8. It's printed on the wedding invitation what we're required to wear.
9. The team that we have to beat is the Wolverines.
10. She is the up-and-coming actress that everyone should watch.

ADJECTIVES FOLLOWED BY PREPOSITIONS

As you've probably seen, prepositions (*for, in, with, by*, etc.) are some of the hardest little words to master in any language. They just need to be memorized, because there's really no rule for how to choose which one is correct. We've already taken a look at some common verbs that take prepositions (*to look at, to worry about, to look forward to . . .*). Now we'll look at some adjectives that take prepositions:

They found the defendant **guilty of** murder.
Sam is **charged with** robbery.
Are you **finished with** the project yet?
I'm really **interested in** Chinese culture.
We're all **curious about** jury duty.
Lana was **exhausted from** running all day.
Are you **familiar with** this poet?
What on earth are you so **angry about**?
Brenda's **angry with** Helen **for** lying to her.
I'm **annoyed with** the kids; they're making too much noise.
You're always **annoyed about** something!
My nephew was **excited about** going to the beach.
Are you **worried about** sharks?
Bill said that he wasn't **afraid of** anything!
Peter is really **bad at** tennis.
Are you any **good at** chess?
We're really **amazed at/by** this weather! It's so windy!
Sigrid's uncle is **famous for** writing books.
Who's **responsible for** writing the report?
We're **involved in** a theater group.
I'm not **convinced of** their story yet.
Silvia was **sorry for** forgetting Sam's birthday.
I'm really **sorry about** your grandmother; you have my condolences.
Don't feel **sorry for** Pete—he's happy that he lost his job!
The author's second book is very **different from** her first.
Please be **patient with** me; I'm a bit slow in the beginning.
It was very **nice of** you to help me with my bags.

*We're very **committed to** our jobs.*
*The Larsons are **proud of** their daughters.*
*We were all **ashamed of** Henry's behavior—he was very rude.*
*Greta is **jealous of** Hiroko; she got a promotion and a new office.*
*Are you **aware of** what's been happening?*
*Paul isn't **capable of** lying!*
*The students are all very **fond of** their teacher.*
*Your responsibilities are **limited to** one account.*
*I'm **tired of** walking. Let's get in a cab.*
*Denise was **absent from** school yesterday. Is she sick?*
*He's been **keen on** traveling to Iceland.*
*My sister is **married to** a guy who works for your company.*
*My mother taught me to be **kind to** people.*
*This song is very **similar to** the last one we heard!*
*The client is **pleased with** the presentation we made.*
*I was very **disappointed with** my score on the test.*
*We're so **bored with** our jobs!*

PRACTICE: ADJECTIVES FOLLOWED BY PREPOSITIONS
Complete each of the following sentences with the proper preposition.

1. The little girl isn't capable _____ lifting that suitcase.
2. We're involved _____ a difficult situation.
3. My boss is angry _____ me _____ coming in late to work so often.
4. Kids, are you finished _____ dinner yet?
5. Jerry's classmates were not kind _____ him.
6. I'm jealous _____ my brother; he has a bigger house and a better job.
7. We need to be patient _____ the new assistant; he'll learn soon enough.
8. David has been absent _____ our class a lot lately.
9. I'm so tired _____ discussing this! Can we take a break?
10. They weren't convinced _____ your argument.
11. This job is similar _____ my last one.
12. What is the person on T.V. famous _____?
13. Dawn is terribly afraid _____ spiders.
14. The team is committed _____ winning this game.
15. The director wasn't aware _____ the problems we had.
16. I'm so bored _____ this movie! Let's go.
17. The fire damage was limited _____ the apartments on the top floor.
18. Everyone is so proud _____ you!
19. I'm sorry, but I'm not familiar _____ this new program.
20. Steven is really excited _____ starting his literature class.

20D LISTENING EXERCISE

🎧 Listen to the recorded sentences and restate them using *get*.

1. *If you're not careful, you'll become sick.*
2. *When did you arrive here?*
3. *Could you have this report copied, please?*
4. *Would you answer the door for me?*
5. *Where can I buy foreign newspapers?*
6. *I'm sorry, I didn't understand your name.*

ANSWER KEY—PRACTICE SECTIONS

VOCABULARY

1. jury
2. attorney
3. stolen
4. sentence
5. curious
6. arrested
7. allegedly
8. defendant
9. Thief
10. duty
11. witnessed
12. charged
13. claimed
14. suspect
15. district attorney
16. theft
17. prosecutes
18. defense attorney
19. judge
20. a bunch of
21. alibi
22. done time
23. trial
24. bail

USES OF GET

1. get serious
2. get off his chest
3. got lost
4. get over
5. get up
6. get in touch
7. get even
8. got back
9. get along with
10. get your way
11. get through
12. get . . . out of
13. get away
14. get through to
15. get away with

NOUN CLAUSES WITH INFINITIVES

1. I don't know what to write.
2. Sarah asked the guard where to go.
3. The kids don't know what to eat.
4. Have you decided where to eat tonight?
5. They keep telling me what to do.
6. Don't tell her what to say to him!
7. Professor Mackenzie told us what to read tonight.
8. It's printed on the wedding invitation what to wear.
9. The team to beat is the Wolverines.
10. She is the up-and-coming actress to watch.

ADJECTIVES FOLLOWED BY PREPOSITIONS

1. of
2. in
3. with . . . for
4. with
5. to
6. of
7. with
8. from
9. of
10. of
11. to
12. for
13. of
14. to
15. of
16. with
17. to
18. of
19. with
20. about

LISTENING EXERCISE

1. If you're not careful, you'll get sick.
2. When did you get here?
3. Could you get this report copied, please?
4. Would you get the door for me?
5. Where can I get foreign newspapers?
6. I'm sorry, I didn't get your name.

Index of Grammatical and Structural Topics

The numbers appearing in parentheses after each item listed refer to the lesson in which the topic can be found

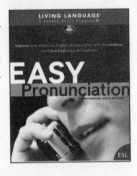